The Twilight of Ideologies

Gonzalo Fernández de la Mora y Mon

Translation of the Salvat edition (1971)
by Thomas Burns Marañón (1974)

Revised for the present edition
by Juan Fernández de la Mora Varela (2024)

The Twilight of Ideologies

Gonzalo Fernández de la Mora y Mon

Translation of the Salvat edition (1971)
by Thomas Burns Marañón (1974)

Revised for the present edition
by Juan Fernández de la Mora Varela (2024)

Academica Press
Washington~London

Library of Congress Cataloging-in-Publication Data

Names: Fernández de la Mora y Mon, Gonzalo (author) | Fernández de la Mora Varela, Juan | Burns, Tom (translator)

Title: The twilight of ideologies | Gonzalo Fernández de la Mora y Mon

Description: Washington : Academica Press, 2025. | Includes references.

Identifiers: LCCN 2024944227 | ISBN 9781680534108 (hardcover) | 9781680534351 (paperback) | 9781680534115 (e-book)

Contents

Preface

When this work was first published in 1965, it argued that scientific approaches were gradually replacing ideologies in the political life of culturally advanced nations. Sixty years later, the present translation of this classic will facilitate the participation of English-speaking readers in a long lived debate that is now particularly relevant in America. The double aim of this prologue is to present the author to English-speaking readers, and to investigate whether his thesis has held true in Europe, the United States, and around the world.

Fernández de la Mora

We thank the illustrious historian Professor Stanley Payne for his permission to introduce our author through the following selected quotes:[1]

> "Gonzalo Fernández de la Mora was the deepest and most original conservative Spanish intellectual of the second half of the 20th century, and one of the most remarkable of that period. He is difficult to classify, as he was a diplomat who lived and worked mainly in Madrid; he was an important figure of Franco's regime who rarely was in government, and a notable philosopher that did not hold an academic post. He intervened in certain key aspects of the politics of the regime; but he always was more an intellectual than a political man, something most uncommon in Franco's Spain."

> "Fernández de la Mora built his own philosophy, not a school, but a personal methodology which he called *razonalismo* –

---

[1] Payne, Stanley review of the book by PEDRO CARLOS GONZÁLEZ CUEVAS: La razón conservadora: Gonzalo Fernández de la Mora, una biografía político-intelectual. Published in Revista de Estudios Políticos (nueva época), Núm. 170, Madrid, octubre-diciembre (2015), págs. 347-349

"reasonalism." This involved the use of reason, not in the Cartesian sense of "pure reason," but as an empirical rationalism applied to current problems. Here one sees the influence of Ortega y Gasset, something that Fernández de la Mora always acknowledged. He never participated in Ortega's rejection, typical of Spanish contemporary conservative writers. He rather stressed that Ortega was fundamentally a conservative, a defensible interpretation, given Ortega's political history, especially after 1936. However, in contrast to Ortega, Fernández de la Mora recognized that, given man's nature, pure reason could not be applied unilaterally. Rather, it always existed in a paradoxical dualism between reason and sentiment."

"Among his books, probably the one best known in his days was *The Twilight of Ideologies*, though perhaps it was also the least understood ... Fernández de la Mora referred to the failures and limitations of the so-called period of ideologies, and proposed their replacement, not by other ideological abstractions, but by rational analysis of existing problems according to empirical and positive criteria, and also coherently with lessons from the past. This directive had been constructed after years of study and reflection."

"Fernández de la Mora entered government in 1970 as head of the Public Works ministry, and defined the regime as an *Estado de obras*, or "Government of Works." His presence in the government ended with the assassination of its Prime Minister, Carrero Blanco. In these years many thought of him as the official thinker of the regime. But his participation in government was relatively brief, and he was heavily criticized from within the system by traditionalists, falangists, as well as by the elements more prone to political change."

"After Franco's death he naturally accepted the need for certain changes. He participated in the transition process first as one of the founders of the political party *Alianza Popular* (now *Partido Popular*). In a second period he abandoned active political life, to devote himself fully to intellectual activities. This last stage of his life was most fruitful, including the publication of his memoirs *Río Arriba* (*Upstream*) and six more books on political and philosophical subjects. He also founded a new journal of serious conservative thought, *Razón Española* (*Spanish Reason*), which is still in good health."

"He was the most complete and sophisticated of all intellectuals formed during Franco's regime."

Is the twilight of ideologies thesis valid today?

A stunning confirmation of the *Twilight of Ideologies'* thesis was seen in Eastern Europe with the Revolutions of 1989 and subsequent collapse of the USSR in 1991. The singularly virulent Marxist-Leninist ideology imploded almost overnight into Russia's current autocratic capitalist regime, and a series of liberal democracies.

The opposite is often thought to have occurred in Western Europe, as the socialist, conservative, and liberal parties continue to dominate. If policy is currently dictated by parties representing each of the major ideologies, how could this possibly be indicative of their twilight? The fact is that the discourse of these parties continuously strays away from their theoretical origins, very much as anticipated by Fernández de la Mora. Furthermore, the convergence in legislation between these supposedly opposing parties clearly demonstrates a gradual departure from ideological thought. The following examples support this notion explicitly:

1) The creation of the French party *En Marche* in 2016 (now *Renaissance*), which brought Macron to the presidency with a clear majority in 2017. *Renaissance* is a centrist party built from the integration of the principal socialist and center right parties in France. A political party unifying the socialist, liberal, and conservative ideologies would have been unthinkable just ten years earlier, yet closely fits the framework promoted by our author in 1965.

2) The European Union Parliament is governed by an alliance of its three major groups: the People's Party (center right), the Socialists & Democrats Party (center left), and Renew Europe (liberal), as the three vote jointly on nearly every occasion. This convergence of political

positions, far beyond that of the corresponding national parties, also fits well the twilight thesis.

3) In the 2024 European Parliament elections in Romania, the Socialist (PSD) and the moderate right party (PNL) formed an electoral coalition, and presented joint candidates with a common set of political objectives: a stunning confirmation of their ideological convergence.

4) Recent developments with the Italian Prime Minister, Giorgia Meloni, further substantiate the convergence of ideologies. Meloni leads the Brothers of Italy party (far right), but since ascending to power she has followed a set of policies similar to those of the European People's Party.

We conclude that the evolution of ideologies in Europe over the last sixty years has clearly followed the pattern announced by Fernández de la Mora: disappearance of the extremist Communist ideology, and convergence of the conservative, liberal and socialist ideologies.

As relates to the United States, in 1965 Fernández de la Mora noted that the Democratic and Republican parties were the least ideological political entities in the world. This suggested that the US was relatively immune to the virus of ideology, but the opposite trend has now taken hold of US culture and politics. Given this clear antithesis, what would be the point of publishing an English translation of this classic? The obvious reason is that much is wrong with the increasing ideologization of the US, and no effort should be spared to reduce it.

This general evaluation is well illustrated by a chief element of American culture. Universities are key centers for the discussion and elaboration of solutions to societal problems. They also used to instill the intellectual habits necessary for the young to contribute to this difficult creative process. However, increasing ideologization of academia is contributing to the opposite. Ideologically driven leaders have achieved an astounding level of control over most cultural institutions, attained by scarcely balanced means. For instance, the right of Yale alumni to nominate Corporation candidates was removed a few years ago by the Corporation. Alumni may still vote, but only Soviet style, for candidates proposed by the administration. Non-Profit cultural institutions, such as private universities, have charters specifying the nature of their social goals. Nevertheless, ideologically driven leaders are corrupting these laboriously built structures to promote rather different goals. A culture enslaved by ideology can hardly maintain its vitality. The ability to think critically, originally, and ethically has long been characteristic of the American people, but the prominence of ideological thought is a formidable barrier to the exertion of these classical virtues. The level to which moral and critical thinking has decayed among leaders of our learned societies was recently simultaneously demonstrated by the inability of the presidents of Harvard, MIT, and UPenn to strike a sensible balance between the absolute evil of genocidal extermination and the good associated to civilized free expression.

We conclude that the present radicalization of ideologies in the US does not match the prognosis of our author. Nevertheless, a key point in his analysis is that ideologies are irrational, and their influence tends to diminish in culturally forward moving societies. The counterexample presently offered by the US is accordingly of the highest relevance. History shows that even the greatest and noblest nations can not only decay, but also be entirely eradicated. It is thus evident that we cannot expect that all societies will always move forward in the desirable path of rationalization and moral purification. The real lesson is that a high cost will follow from moving backwards along that road, and that ideology is one of the great drivers of that retrograde evolution. We thus hope that the US edition of this classic will contribute to the needed regeneration of American culture. A first step in that direction is to forget for a moment whether this or that ideology is right or wrong, and to describe all ideologies generically by their true substance: an intellectual detritus that substitutes the scientific analysis of real social problems by a primitive and passionately held prejudice on magic formulae presumed to resolve all issues, irrespective of circumstances. This generic debunking of the ideological way of thinking is brilliantly carried out by Fernández de la Mora in this essay.

If we turn our attention to the remaining nations of the world, the analysis of a present-day *twilight of ideologies* is more nuanced. As a confirmation of our author's thesis, we can highlight the case of China: the communist ideology has been in retreat for decades, even as the CCP remains an authoritarian power. Today China is much better defined as a capitalist country led by communists than as a communist country, and its remaining ideology is steadily converging towards Western ideals. On the opposite viewpoint, religion's increasing role in world politics was not factored in by our author, and the rise of Islamic fundamentalism has been a pivotal argument against his twilight prediction. However, these retrograde developments do confirm our author's sociological principle on the tight connection between increased ideologization and cultural decay.

The present translation, the first published in English, is based on the popular 1971 Spanish Salvat edition. Of the many editions available in various languages, the most recent is a critical scholarly version edited by Carlos Goñi Apesteguia (OLMS, 2013). It includes a detailed introduction and numerous notes, but exists only in Spanish.

Juan and Gonzalo Fernández de la Mora Varela
July 1, 2024

About the Author

BIOGRAPHY. One of Spain's most distinguished philosophers, Gonzalo Fernández de la Mora y Mon was born in Barcelona on April 30, 1924. He graduated in law and philosophy from the University of Madrid with the highest distinction in both subjects and then entered the Spanish diplomatic corps, serving in West Germany and Greece and as head of the Diplomatic School of Spain. In 1950, he married Isabel Varela, with whom he had four children. In 1953, Fernández de la Mora y Mon began a lengthy collaboration with the conservative monarchist daily *ABC*. From 1970 to 1974, he served as Spain's Minister of Public Works and later held a seat in parliament. He became a member of Spain's Royal Academy of Political and Moral Sciences in 1972. In 1983, he founded the bimonthly journal *Razón Española*, a publication devoted to the defense of a humanistic world view. He died at home on February 10, 2002.

A summary of his exceptional merits is not easily made. He greatly enjoyed hunting for antiques. For instance, he assembled one of the best Spanish collections of antique silver, which he donated to the Museum of Pontevedra. To enrich his vast culture, he collected what would probably be the last large Spanish library, which he gave in life to the Academy of Moral and Political Sciences. He was a brilliant public speaker, and a feared polemist. He published his first book at age 19, the novel *Paradoj*a (1944). His unique literary style earned him the Spanish National Literature award in 1961, the Spanish National Art and Essay Price (1970) and the Spain Mirror Price (1995) for his autobiography *Rio Arriba* (*Upstream*). In politics he was coauthor of one piece of the Constitution (Ley Orgánica del Estado). He was a member of parliament, both before and during the elaboration of the current Spanish Constitution. His final political act was his vote against this Constitution because of its predictable dissolving effects on national unity. He was Director of the Spanish Diplomatic School, and during his last ten years before retirement was number one in the professional hierarchy of the diplomatic corps. As a journalist, he headed *ABC*'s section of Collaborations, directed its literary pages, and was literary critic. He received the following journalism awards: Premio Mariano de Cavia, Premio Luca de Tena, Premio Julio Camba y Premio Gibraltar Español.

The leading aspect of Fernández de la Mora was his intellectual activity. As an independent thinker with a footing on the classics, he framed his work on the most current ideas of conservative thought, European (especially German) and North American, without concessions to the varying tides of Spanish politics. He published 22 books, 14 shorter works, and 116 studies. Leading among them are *The Twilight of Ideologies* (1965), *Pensamiento español* (7 volumes, 1964-1970), *Egalitarian Envy* (1984; available in English translation, with a more accurate translation soon to appear) and *On Happiness* (2001). Translations of his books exist in Italian, Portuguese, French, English, German and Greek.

SCHOLARLY CONTRIBUTIONS. The writings of Fernández de la Mora encompass a broad range of subjects, from literature to literary criticism, though his contributions in the theory of government and in philosophy are perhaps the most noteworthy. In the former, his ideas have led to radical advances, especially through works such as *The Twilight of Ideologies*, *Partitocracy*, *Egalitarian Envy*, and *From the Ideal State to the State of Reason*.

The Twilight of Ideologies dwelled on the convergence of ideologies, the rationalization of politics, and the strong link between ideologization and cultural decay.

La partitocracia (Partitocracy) is of comparable current interest, especially in political systems lacking an independent President. According to the theory of the *general will*, the function of a parliament is to approach truth through debate. But decisions in the modern parliament are made outside of the chambers by the heads of the parties. The party oligarchy also selects and controls the candidates to the chambers, who cannot therefore vote according to either their conscience or the mandate of their electors. Furthermore, the increasing power of the parties has canceled the principle of separation of powers by direct interference in judicial appointments. The parties are accordingly oligarchic organizations, making a myth of the principle of government of the people by the people.

Egalitarian Envy starts with a fascinating account of the views expressed about this passion by leading thinkers, including the author himself. Envy is born through the perception of the superior happiness of another. The envious subject then reacts by attempting to debase the envied object. In politics, this destructive sentiment is channeled through the abasement of those above, conveniently attained through the requirement of equality. This passion is therefore the driving force behind the appeal of egalitarian parties. Its antidote is emulation, the positive will to achieve what one desires by lifting oneself, rather than lowering the other. Egalitarian envy thus obstructs the process of putting the right man in the right place, affecting most negatively the efficiency of social organizations.

Del Estado ideal al Estado de Razon (From the Ideal State to the State of Reason). In *The Twilight of Ideologies*, Fernández de la Mora rejects the utopian ideological approach to judge a government irrespective of its success, by its similarity to an ideal standard (communism, socialism, liberalism, etc.). What alternative means should one then use to evaluate a political system? The author notes that the State has not been created to satisfy a certain theoretical standard of beauty and harmony. Rather, it is an instrument created by men to handle fundamental social problems insoluble by individual citizens. But the notion of an ideal instrument is nonsense without a reference to its function (to cut, to hammer, to squeeze), which in turns depends entirely on the circumstances of the task at hand (to cut a lemon, or an oak, or a steel bar, etc.). Fernández de la Mora defines the key functions of the state as achieving order, dispensing justice, and promoting development. A good state, like a good instrument, is the one which in practice achieves well the function for which it was created.

"**REASONALISM.**" Fernández de la Mora initiated in 1982 a philosophical movement called *razonalismo*, first through his editorials in

Razon Española (to be collected in book form under the title *El buho de Minerva,* or *Minervas's Owl*), and also through his deeply anthropological books *La envidia igualitaria* (*Egalitarian Envy*) and *Sobre la Felicidad* (*On Happiness*). The essence of the movement is the application of reason to all areas of human life, especially its intellectual and moral dimensions. In the former, he uses the pathos/logos (sentiment/reason) dualism to reinterpret several leading Spanish philosophers (Zubiri, Amor Ruibal, Ortega y Gasset, D'Ors, García Morente and Millán Puelles), commending and criticizing respectively their rational and their irrational element. On the moral front, he elaborates an ethics where good and evil do not simply follow from tradition or revelation, but from rational analysis based on the wellbeing of humankind. What follows from this postulate is, broadly speaking, the stoic ideal of the *mastery of the self*, though not that of *impassibility*. Not all sentiments are adverse. Much the opposite, some, such as compassion and the love for one's neighbor are splendid. The predominant existential rule is not so much to live according to the logos, but to feel according to reason. Neither renouncing the world or being indifferent to it, nor passively being driven by appetites. Rather, to desire and to feel reasonably.

RAZÓN ESPAÑOLA. In 1983, Fernández de la Mora founded the journal *Razón Española* (*Spanish Reason*) which has become the main organ of Spanish conservative thought. Along its main lines of action have been the following:
	-Exposition of the author's philosophical system, *Razonalismo.* First in its personal facet as a guide for human life. And also in its public facet, especially on leading public issues of the day, from the fall of the Berlin Wall to globalization.
	-Defense of the positive aspects of Spanish history, and in particular Franco's Spain, given its exceptional achievements in areas such as economic development, social justice, convergence with Europe, political honesty and rule of law.
	-Defense of cosmopolitanism, and other processes of integration, particularly the European Union, and a concomitant criticism of disintegrating nationalisms, especially those contributing now and

then to the collapse of Spanish unity.

-Criticism of *partitocracy*, including measures to moderate party powers, to help nations having fallen into this oligarchic system better approach the liberal paradigm.

-Design of a new state for the next millenium, characterized by technification, depolitization, decentralization, liberalization, and more direct democratic forms

SUMMARY. Gonzalo Fernández de la Mora Varela was undoubtedly the leading Spanish conservative thinker of the twentieth century. He created an important body of doctrine in political theory, as well as in philosophy. His precocious announcements on such matters as ideologies, political parties, or the passion driving egalitarianism provide ample evidence for the clarity of his vision. Nevertheless, it is inappropriate to describe the man without stressing that most important in his life was the rectitude and coherence of his trajectory as a person. Behind his work lies a human person with an exemplary behavior, who left numerous friends without political or social distinctions, and who sowed among those that knew him the same high values for which he lived.

I. Anticipations

The Subject

Social contemporary life has been dominated by ideologies. In the programs of candidates and governments, dictators and revolutionaries, there has been a predominance of the ideological content. Mass movements and opinion makers have also been driven by ideologies. The signs of weakness of this vast, long-lived, and strong empire had not begun to be worrying until past the end of World War II. Very recently, certain negative symptoms have multiplied and increased in strength. One of the most striking has been the progressive substitution of ideologies by technical and economic plans in government programs. For example, here are the goals proposed by the head of the British labor party in 1963: to form a greater number of scientist, to utilize them more intelligently, and to apply most vigorously to industry the results of scientific research. The ships of the state are changing direction.

Why one studies a subject is a complex and intimate question; but the reasons why one publishes a book must at this time in history be justified. Tons of printing ink are used daily in broad areas of the western World. And the disciplines still counting with a readily digestible bibliography are now rare. The truth is that there are too many materials, either known, or mediocre, or previously published, which only serve to increase and muddy the stream of printed letter. To satisfy a desire of vain glory or of catharsis is not sufficient reason to tempt the reader with a new title. I would not have dared to put black over white my reflections about the crisis of ideologies had I not stumbled recently, abruptly, and repeatedly with the pertinacious blindness of many Spaniards, even intellectuals, who persist not just in resuscitating anachronic panaceas, but in centering the political life of their compatriots within the dying dialectic of ideologies. They are the stimulus and the reason for this book. Will they realize that ideologism is presently reactionarism and a return to situations in their way to disappearance? It is worth trying, directly and briefly. A new understanding of politics begins to appear in the horizons of the pioneering intellectuals. Let us not stubbornly ignore it.

Much has already been written about ideologies, and a little, though contradictory, about their decline. The present absence of the notes that overload some of my other studies, mean neither a pretension of originality, nor disrespect for the sources. I am astronomically distant from either. But to describe with sober lines a phenomenon as vast and contemporary as the agony of ideologies, the testimony of others seems unnecessary to me. And to support polemic conclusions, it is more sportive to avoid the crutches of the authoritative testimony. What follows is a sincere and humble personal struggle with the subject.

The Thesis

Throughout this meager study I try to analyze, with some systematism and rigor, a phenomenon complex but solitary: the twilight of ideologies. Each and all of the lines converge towards a focal point. The data complement each other, and the reasonings condition each other. It is a thematic monopoly and a Robinsonic conceptual monarchy. The effort is also governed by a sustained intentional unity and by a single driving force. The accessory and marginal achieves its meaning by being rooted on the substantial and basic: the experience of the decay of ideologies. Nevertheless, the central thesis is split into two planes: the facts and the principles. We start from the facts. Ideologies are factors of social tension; but we live in a period of political apathy and relaxation. Ideologies are extremist and pugnacious; but we witness a liberal-socialist amalgam. Ideologies are pathetic and mythic; but politics and life are being rationalized. Ideologies are related to beliefs; but religions interiorize and purify themselves. Ideologies proliferate within the modest cultural strata, as well as at critical economic junctions; yet we face an era of fabulous cultural and material development. The events and the tendencies most prominent at present go against the development of ideologies. What is decisive is not that they decay; it is that circumstances will be progressively less favorable, and that this evolution appears as irreversible. These are the facts, and the implicit anticipation for the future. Besides these dominant circumstances, a fraternal element of a normative nature begins to configure itself: the lesson that one must accelerate as much as possible the process of substituting ideologies for the concrete ideas contributed by ethics and the social sciences. This preceptive deduction is empirically backed: if ideologies are linked to tension, pugnacious and utopic extremism, politicization of intimacy, irrationality, and underdevelopment, and if these five situations are of negative sign, would it make sense to consolidate ideological currents? The clear answer is no, and it streams from reality, very much as reality manifests itself. It is an "ought to be" which emerges from "what is." It is the minimal expression of an a priori, and as close as possible to a causal relation.

Two Prior Objections

The extinction of ideology seems to imply a sort of political unanimity, and therefore, the end of dissonances and pluralism. The first would be utopic because differences of both opinion and of interest are consubstantial with social life. The second would be counterproductive because debate is the nerve of dialectics, and the collision of different intentions is what drives groups. Would the suppression of ideological tensions be the end of political entropy and something close to social death? This objection has, among other deficiencies, it's ignorance of the facts. For there are centuries of effective history without ideologies. Furthermore, the objection falsely pretends the reduction of all social plurality to that strictly ideological. Natural sciences progress impelled by dialogue between their practitioners and by comparison of hypotheses with reality, generally, without ideology. Why couldn't political scientists progress similarly? Ideological fights, due to their passional, simplistic and latitudinarian character, are not particularly favorable to synthesis, clarification, and dialogue. They are not properly hermeneutic but hardening processes. Besides ideological pluralism, there is the pluralism of ideas, which is what animates authentic intellectual life. If equality is a value, its sociological condition, homogeneity, would also be a value. Another thing would be the complete unification and absolute unanimity, situations as impossible as of improbable fecundity.

The second objection is of far greater weight: what hidden ideological charge hides behind a criticism of ideologies? From Marx's times, especially after Manheim, the great obsession of cultural sociologists and of all suspicious readers has been to guess the prejudices of the author, the interests he defends, the principles from which he proceeds, the sentiments moving him, that is, the impure, what misguides reasoning and deforms reality. Some believe that a new ideology hides behind positions contrary to the great ideologies of the day: technocratism. The term is confusing; but in its most pejorative meaning it implies ignorance of the social sciences, and a hegemony of applications over research, and of practice over theory. There is a pretension of establishing a parallelism between the non-ideological politician and the mechanical engineer. One must note first that criticizing ideologies, even in the name of technocracy, is a speculative endeavor, and therefore, to a large measure philosophical. It is not exclusively empirical, because it has axiological dimensions, and it is not physical but humanistic. Furthermore, as a result of their simplistic slogans of immediate application, ideologies are rather far from scientific purity. In this sense, the handymen and artisans are rather the ideologues than those who seek an authentic rationalization of knowledge and of the public activity. It is not a question of judging an ideology from another: to attack liberalism to defend socialism. What one attains finally is a general negative evaluation. On the other hand, ideologies are not condemned due to their greater or lesser falsity, but through their very nature, for being ideologies, namely degenerative underproducts of a vulgarized and pathetic mental activity. They are not genuine ideas, and this distinction is absolutely essential: it is the key to all the present argument. The final condemnation of ideologies is not made under the protection of a moral imperative, but from a logical principle: they are pseudo ideas. And the diagnostic of their crisis is based on the bare facts.

The proposed solution is not technocracy, but "ideocracy." It is not a new ideologism, but a plain anti-ideologic position. It is not a deintellectualization, but a superintellectualization of social life. It is not a dehumanization, but an exaltation of the most human, because it is proper to man to operate, not just by instinct or emotions, but also according to rational ideas. These are the supreme and absolute weapons. Taking ideologies apart is not an endeavor for technocrats, but rather for those who struggle to subject social life to the sovereignty of rigorous and exact ideas. They do not denounce a certain axiom or a concrete pretension, but the fraud of giving noble theoretical appearance to an alloy of conceptual detritus and sentiments. The issue is to raise the level and is, in sum, a different world. This is what we must now prove.

II. Towards a Definition

All political terms are simultaneously names of things, masks, and throwing weapons. They are situated at the meeting point of interests and passions. The harsh treatment of doctrinaires, statesmen, demagogues, and the plebs deforms and wears them out. They follow a painful and triumphant path of semantic volatilization. They appear to be cruelly destined to walk towards complete amphibology and loss of all proper meaning. After almost three millennia of manipulation, who knows the meaning of "democracy"? Fortunately, "ideology" is linguistically almost a newborn, and though much travelled, it preserves some stabilizing and determining edges. To make progress, it is essential to prospect the field and anchor the term in a fixed meaning.

Four Interpretations

Although a modern term, the word ideology is ambiguous. Some of its meanings are so different from each other that they have hardly anything in common. In order to approach the subject with any degree of exactness, it is therefore necessary to ascertain our terms. We must distinguish between the science of ideas, a prejudice, an epiphenomenon, and vulgarized philosophy.

1) Ideology was a Hellenic term that was resurrected by Destrutt de Tracy in a brief note in the introduction to his *Elements*. He defined it etymologically as the science of ideas. The philosophy of this disciple of Condillac was sensualism. Starting from the premise that superior psychical phenomena originated in the senses, Destrutt de Tracy concluded that ideas were composed of sensations and that thinking was equivalent to feeling. Such empiricism placed him in a position hostile to classical psychology and consequently to the traditional conception of the world. In religion the ideologues were agnostics and in politics they were liberals. That is why, when Napoleon turned his back on his revolutionary principles and established a dictatorship, he saw in the ideologues a form of doctrinal opposition to his regime, and therefore declared war on their *tenebreuse metaphysique*. The politically pejorative meaning of ideologies springs from this Bonapartist opposition.

A second philosophical school attempted to rehabilitate the term by freeing it from its sensualist connections. Thus, Balmes termed pure ideology that part of metaphysics which had as its object pure intellectual order. Balmes' reinterpretations, directed precisely against the empiricism of Condillac and Destrutt de Tracy, while contributing to a less partisan and more generic acceptance of the term, were not however generally adopted.

2) A second meaning complicated matters. There is a fundamental preoccupation in all philosophy: one must abandon prejudices in order to indulge in pure thinking. This is the obsessive concern of modern critical thought. With his theory of *idols and prejudices* Bacon gave it a striking and fruitful formulation. He defined idola as erroneous notions that were formed by a man's biological, social, or cultural condition, and that hindered the search for truth. Idola were inherited fallacies that clouded

understanding. So, modern rationalism places all the innumerable beliefs traditions and opinions, which by the 19th Century began to be known as ideologies, in the category of idols and prejudices. In this way the term acquired a philosophically negative meaning. Ideology became synonymous with a conviction that was not authentic, that was irrational and ultimately false.

3) It was however Marx who weakened both the theory and practice of ideologies. Already in 1758 Helvetius had written "Our ideas are the necessary consequences of the age in which we live." Marx reduced ideas to the simple condition of epiphenomena, that is the result of a basic and ulterior situation, in his case the socioeconomic relationship. He declared that "the mode of production of material life conditions the process of social, political, and spiritual existence." In short, so called superstructures, *ueberbau*, whether institutions or ideologies, depended on the economic structures, that is on the modes of production. The deduction from this is that philosophy, law, morality, art, and religion are mere sub-products that in part reflect and in part attempt to sublimate or justify simple group interests. Ideas and aesthetic forms are therefore epiphenomena, manifestations of economic and social tensions. They are in short ideologies.

The identification of ideologies with propaganda came as an inevitable variant of the Marxist interpretation. If they are unable to have a pretention of absolute truth, ideologies are inherently false. When the will to give a rational justification and an apologetic explanation of an unjust situation is conscious, like the defense of a criminal, they are a mask, a deformation, and a sophism. It is nevertheless evident that the presentation of ideologies as lies requires a study, not from the perspective of human groups, but from that of individuals, since these are the only capable to knowingly lie. This problem is more ethical and psychological than sociological.

In the Marxian thesis and the later one of Dilthey, concepts are historical, that is, are subject to a dependence on time. This premise has given rise to a very modern discipline, the sociology of knowledge. Its object is the study of thought in relation to the socio-economic conditions in which it was formulated. Scheler, Manheim and Geiger have been the leaders of this school. According to it, ideologies are important, not so much because of their truth, but as reflections or symptoms of any given social structure. The Marxist and historicist origins of the sociology of knowledge and of some of its most eminent proponents does not however signify that this discipline necessarily presupposes materialism or relativism.

4) There is a fourth meaning that is a final precipitate of all the former ones. According to it, an ideology is a *simplified and vulgarized political philosophy*. The epistemological problem is left aside. It does not matter whether ideologies are prejudices or epiphenomena or neither, nor the extent of their truth. Although the veracity of ideologies parallels that of the conceptual system giving rise to them, that is a critical question which we cannot here undertake. The concept that is obtained must be equally valid for Marxist and Christian ideologies. It is the simple existence of ideologies that interests us here, not their affirmative content. In their strictest sense ideologies are the popular and pragmatic version of a system of ideas. They can therefore become a program for communal life, and ultimately a political credo. Liberalism, socialism, and communism are considered today as living ideologies. From this perspective, they are the object of our study.

Ideologies and Ideas

Ideologies are not tangible realities such as a range of hills. Rather, like algebra, they belong to the realm of thought. Predominantly they contain principles for action and behavioral norms, in the same way as do logic and morality. They are therefore a class or type of idea, since one cannot think or act rationally without having ideas. An ideology is an amalgam of concepts, judgments and reasonings, but it is a peculiar one. There is a distinction between what is ideological and what is strictly scientific. A dry definition cannot clarify this dichotomy; it must be approached in a roundabout way.

First precision. An ideology is a practical, not a theoretical knowledge. Theoretical knowledge such as metaphysics does not presuppose any action and sees pure knowledge as its only end. An ideology leads directly to the execution of acts, the adoption of decisions and modes of conduct. They are fertile and spectacular, and are always reflected in external history. They are the agents provocateurs of programs and operations. As a result, the nerve-end of every ideology is always a series of recommendations or precepts.

Second precision. The implicit norms of any ideology are not rules of conscience such as the command to love God. They concern the citizen, the man in society and not the solitary man. They attempt to order men's lives jointly on earth. Ideologies seek to form a basis for the polity, and so necessarily become a program for government and the structuring of society. Ideologies aspire to be the ferment of constitutional law and social morality.

Third precision. An ideology is however neither morality nor rigorous political science in the exact sense of those terms. For some doctrinaires, an ideology can be the object of a more or less scientific treatment and justification. This is the case of Marx's socialism. But there remains in all cases an irresistible urgency for practice and a high degree of popularization. Unlike calculus, an ideology is a mental product for the consumption of the masses. It is not even an originally esoteric discipline, such as astronomy, later adapted and vulgarized. An ideology is born for the humbler strata of humanity. It is conceived for the underdeveloped markets of human thoughts. It is the ante-chamber of collective action and the spur of social movements.

Fourth precision. The plebeian element in ideologies does not deprive them of their condition of ideas. But it does make those ideas simplistic and sensationalist. The socialist who preaches egalitarianism does not stop to explain how the innate differences between blacks and whites, geniuses and mediocrities are to be overcome. The liberal who propagates the government of the people by the people does not explain the mathematical formulae which will account for the electoral coefficients in system of proportional representation. It is not that ideologies do not descend from the level of principles. It is just that, were they not always facile and propagandistic, they would fail. An ideology does not progressively become more concrete and structured in the way that a scientific discipline develops. Instead, it concentrates on key words, whose content becomes increasingly more general and extremist.

Fifth precision. Ideologies, even when they are originally the work of intellectuals, and so the product of reason, acquire, as they become popularized, the characteristics of a belief. They become received beliefs that the believer does not question. If he is forced to defend himself in a polemic, he does so with mechanical arguments or with personal sentiments. One has ideas, but where ideology is concerned, one is part of them. Ideologies are not reasoned, they are affirmed, lived, felt, and transmitted; socialism is good and that is all there is to it. An ideology is not a meditation, but an illusion; not a conviction but a situation; not a conclusion but a passion. An established ideology resembles a myth more than anything else.

Sixth precision. There is moreover a sacralization of ideologies. They become crystallized into dogmatic passwords and intangible hypotheses. One is either for them or against them. To abandon them is apostasy, and to reform them constitutes heretical deviationism. As in religious conceptions, they ultimately condition everything. This is the case of communism; nothing escapes its tutelage, from biology to metallurgy. Ideologies in their prime are lay gospels, secularized dogmas. They have their prophets and their martyrs, and they are the prime causes of the most violent international tensions and wars. As sacred as the Koran is for Islam was the Declaration of the Rights of Man of 1789 for the demo-liberals, and the Manifesto of 1848 for the socialists.

Seventh precision. Ideologies concern themselves with ultimate goals rather than with immediate stages. They avoid the minutiae of technical and bureaucratic details. They do not therefore usually contain details on the procedure to be followed in order to achieve what is desired. Exceptionally, when they make long-term policy decisions, they do so in very general drafts, which later need constant reappraisals. This is the case with the universal Marxist slogan of the nationalization of the means of production. How public property is to be administered is not established, nor have socialist governments been able in practice to inflexibly maintain the nationalizing policy. The case of liberalism and the vote provides an analogous situation. Ideologies oscillate between the utopia and the panacea. The ideological is rarely honestly realist.

It is not therefore a question of ideologies not being ideas. They are, but they are pragmatic, political, popular, elemental, generalized, emotional, dogmatic, and utopian. Nor is it a question of ideologies being inherently and absolutely false. Their degree of falseness and exaggeration depends on their fidelity to the philosophical systems that nurtured them, and the greater or lesser veracity of these. Even what was originally just and exact, as it is turned into an ideology, becomes radicalized and deformed. At best ideologies are reasonings that are caricatured and corrupted after an intense process of logical and psychological extrapolation and ultimately of massification.

Opinion and Ideology

When one says ideology, one speaks of what is neither rigorous science nor strict knowledge. This distinction between certain knowledge and problematic knowledge, between what is exact and what is approximate, what is reason and what is improvised, what is pure and what has an interest at stake, is as old as speculative philosophy. It more or less corresponds to the division between wise and ignorant men. When 2,600 years ago philosophy was born, Parmenides of Elea, the father of metaphysics, divided his poetry into two forms, corresponding to the two paths of knowledge: the path of truth or *aletheia* and the path of opinion or *doxa*. For this great poet-thinker, opinion was a plebeian knowledge that was not necessarily true. This lesson remains alive today. The most brilliant minds of every age have transmitted in an increasingly elaborate form the Parmenidian message, and they have converted it into one of the most inflexible constants of western thought.

This contraposition is also the nucleus of Platonic philosophy. *Doxa* or opinion is changeable, not very clear, susceptible to error and unintelligent. It is opposed by *epistema* or science in its truest sense. Equally, Aristotle defined opinion as "knowledge that can be wisdom or ignorance." Throughout history, great minds have confirmed this sentence. Hegel took the conclusion to its limits: "Philosophy has no room for opinion. Philosophic opinions do not exist, only certainties exist." This was the end of a millenary process: opinion is a proscribed position for intellectuals.

The average man generally knows for certain what he wants and what hinders or favors the satisfaction of his desires. These simple, clear coordinates orient his life. But when dealing with questions of theory and principle, only the scientist can be certain. This favorable situation occurs of course only in areas in which the scientist is a specialist. In other domains, like the immense majority of people, he also depends on opinions and beliefs. The jurisdictions of inferior rational knowledge are therefore very wide. For centuries, science has been the exception. Historical humanity has lived at a relatively low logical level. The purely external greatness of opinion is due to the fact that it has always prevailed quantitatively to a very great extent over science.

Let us attempt an outline of the concept by distinguishing it from the three notions closest to it. An opinion is not a "faith" because it is earthly and rationally understandable. A faith is supernatural and inaccessible to reason. Nor is it "a belief," that is, a conviction never personally verified by those who live by it. There are many who believe in Pythagoras' theorem without being able to prove it. Instead, inherent in an opinion is the suspicion that the opposite might be true. "I am of the opinion" is not synonymous with "I believe," but with "I think." Nor can an opinion be identified as a hypothesis. In every hypothetical judgement a supposition is proposed that is neither affirmed nor denied, and which can always be cast aside. An opinion is, however, characterized by a pretention to truth, and there are many who retract their opinions when their facts are shown to be in error. In conclusion, faith is supernatural, belief is irrational, hypothesis is rational but not affirmative, and opinion is an imperfect and irregular expression of reason. In the abstract, it is a degeneration, but in concrete form it is an expedient denoting urgency.

In the formation of opinions haste is a decisive factor. We make an opinion when we need an idea but lack any scientific certitude. Man is a thinking animal and life sometimes places him in a situation when he has to improvise a conceptual solution. Then, lacking time, inspiration, and strength, he is reduced to forming opinions.

From the existential perspective, opinions manifest themselves as emergency exits, improvised recourses, and compromises between the will and the intellect, substitutes for real knowledge. Opinions respond to man's intellectual condition and to his inherent pride. That is why the man who opines has neither the peace of mind of a believer, nor the detached irony of the man who formulates a hypothesis. There is only the rushed and anguished attachment of one who needs a weapon, and grasps the best that lies within reach. An opinion is not a faith enabling a man to survive, nor is it an act of confidence, nor a substitute for thought. It is an instrument for life.

When opinions are shared by great numbers and concern common interests, they cease to be an individual operation and, being collectivized, they acquire a special virulence. They become strong and outgoing, and, on occasions, they become stabilized within a program. They are then no longer a face-saving, private artifact, and extend their vigilance in time and space. They become transformed into the liberating panaceas of a group. And because they know that they can be contradicted by other opinions, they become militant. Ideologies are simply collective opinions that concern the common good. In addition to the deficiency of the primitive form of knowledge inherent to *doxa*, one has to note additional ones: utopianism, lack of authenticity, and sectarianism. As the vacuum of an evidence is filled by an opinion, the vacuum in the social sciences is filled by an ideology, that is, by a vulgarized and radicalized collective opinion concerning the state.

All this means that, when an ideology confronted by rigorous political science receives a pejorative significance, no intellectual juggling is at work. One is simply applying in a concrete case a key distinction which, since Parmenides, structures all knowledge: that between opinion and science.

The Function of Tension

An atmosphere of mutual tolerance is rather similar to the notion in physics of fields (magnetic, gravitational), and registers two polarized situations: that of balance and that of movement. The balance in such an atmosphere is dynamic, not static, it is the permanence of an order that is always identical to itself. It is a purely speculative term because historically social life is in constant alteration. The movement which in sociology is known as "change" is the distance between two limiting positions, peaceful tolerance, and total anarchy. In other words, between absolutely ordered and absolutely disordered change. Between these two extremes, which are hypothetical and not factual possibilities, there are innumerable intermediate positions. A warmongering peace and a Cold War are two sides of the same coin. With the necessary terminological modifications, the same outline is as valid on a national as on an international scale. The speed and volume of social change depends on the intensity of the forces present. In a situation of relaxed tolerance, the process is evolutionary. In one where a high tension exists, any movement can be revolutionary. With tension there is risk. Without it, neither life nor progress are possible. Tension is therefore a desirable danger, and to a lesser or greater extent, inevitable.

The two major factors in social tension are interests and ideologies. Their respective modes of action are very different. Interests concern possessions of an economic character. The man who acts under the motivation of an interest is calculating and realistic; his internal motivation allows him to make concessions and bargains, enabling formulae for compromise. Instead, ideologies are essentially maximalist; they must be so in order to realize themselves fully. Ideological authenticity is synonymous with avocation for the extreme. In short, ideologies are by their nature integrist.

Like "liberal," "pronunciamiento" and "fifth column," "integrism" is a word that Spain has given to the political lexicon. It is not a senseless and popular catch phrase, for it has documented and cultured origins. The word was coined by Ramón Nocedal when he founded the "Integrist" Party in 1898. His program outlined a theocratic state, inquisitorial, republican, and entirely subject to the temporal and religious instructions of Rome.

It is not, however, infrequent for proper names to gain popular acceptance, above all, when they concern the state. The use and abuse of political terms generalizes them in addition to wearing them out. Integrist, fascist, radical, are not solely the names of specific historical groups and programs. They are also abstract concepts. Integrism no longer means loyalty to Nocedal's extinct political party, but a certain quality that any political party can adopt, whatever its specific program might be. It is a mood within which any conviction can be held, nationalization or private ownership, centralism, or regionalism. Integrism attempts to reduce what is complex to simple terms, even at the risk of mutilating and caricaturing a concept. It denies subtle distinctions and precision, it is utopian and extremist, insensitive to circumstantial modifications and the limits of reality. It is also radical and totalitarian because it seeks the ultimate consequences and renounces containment, the middle way, the lesser evil and tolerance. It is also dogmatic and accuses all dissidents of disloyalty and heresy, eliminating reason and dialogue. Its favorite denunciation is treason. Ultimately, it is tolerance reduced to the absurd, the exaltation of fanaticism, passion, blind obedience, and enthusiasm. As a fundamental attitude it is very far from the intellectual mood, which implies objectivity, subtlety, open mindedness, and rationalism. An integrist ideology is the complete opposite of an interest because it precludes negotiation.

Integrisms have not died, for they are the natural end of every ideology. Mao Tse Tung is the head of Marxist integrism. The Ku Klux Klan is a form of racist nationalism in an overdeveloped country. It has innumerable parallels in the Afro-Asian world. The 19th century was rich in extreme democratic formulae. "Let liberty be established though the heavens should fall." In Spain, what was then known as left wing integrism, has been one of the classic attitudes of political and intellectual life. Anarchism is the ultimate position of the integrist who seeks total independence.

All integrisms are philistine and this is particularly true of those of a revolutionary kind. They eventually end in negativism, violence, and error. History is full of frightening examples of this, from Marat to Stalin. The tactical skill of those movements consists in labelling their opponents as integrist. But that dialectic is not correct nor can be correct, because there are no reactionary, entrenched integrists: they are all aggressive and expansionist. Today's integrist tendencies are not generally found in traditional groups, which have been penetrated by empiricism and methodological doubts through a combination of prudence and historical experience. They are to be found instead in the newer and more youthful sectors. Nor do they appear among good believers of a religion, but among the henchmen of ideologies.

In contrast to the compromise that is essential to interests, ideologies lean towards integrism. They respond to a mechanism that is in part logical and in part passionate, that is inflexible and repudiates give and take. It is either all or nothing. There is no compromise between truth or error, love or hate. Ideologies will not be submitted to an economic valuation which would leave room for negotiation. They admit no bargains and are resistant to any arithmetical operation. Between two healthy ideologies one cannot achieve a compromise. There is a gradation that orders hierarchically the different ideologies. As they are more utopian, so they create more tension. Communism constitutes today the most forceful vector in the social field. It is the absolute character of an ideology that determines its greatness and its misery.

Interests are very susceptible to juridical protection, and so to peaceful compatibility. Ideological demands, on the other hand, are not. That is why violence, the class struggle and war, is their normal outcome. Civil strife caused by the explosion of internal pressures is not brought about by interests but by ideologies. This was the case of the war of succession, of the Carlist wars and of the civil war in Spain. It was the case of the European revolutions of 1848. It was also the case of all international conflicts, from the Crusades to the last World War, including the religious wars. For half a century the champions of historical materialism have tried to show the economic motivation of human life and therefore of its struggles. But the thesis is unacceptable as much in the general as in the concrete case of a particular struggle. In the monumental "Study of War" edited by Wright, the chapter on the motivation of war concludes: "they are cultural, religious, and political motives; ideals such as the family, the Church and the Nation; sentiments that are not born of reason, but from the most profound part of the personality." There are some who die for a plate of lentils, but there are millions who have given their life for a symbol, a passion, or a myth. The capacity for generating excitement is infinitely more present in ideologies than in interests. The former are the cause of the bloodiest social movements.

There remains the question of whether interests give birth to an ideology. If they do, then the distinction that has been made has only a passing value. Man, being the ethical animal that he is, seeks to justify his desires. And among the root of all ideologies there are barely disguised interests. But there are a multitude of interests that do not give rise to an ideology. Among them are those that are essentially individual, since the desires for esoteric objects corresponding to very personal tastes are not susceptible to generalization. They cannot therefore be the basis of ideologies, which are by definition created for a mass audience. The number of individual interests is far superior to that of common ones. But in any case, even the more universal interests do not need an ideological basis. Perhaps the most shared of our interests is the possession of the other sex. It is precisely in this area where the sense of sin is most frequent. The most generalized state of mind in the human race, including those who are religiously agnostic, is the consciousness of culpability. Yet these dramatic situations would be impossible if we succeeded at justifying all our interests. In such a situation there would only be a continued state of grace and clear conscience. To affirm that all interests give rise to an ideology is to deny man's moral condition and all the evidence that exists for it.

To conclude, there are some interests that are justified by an ideology, there are many that we see as contrary to any form of justification, namely as illegitimate interest, and there are many that are justified not by an ideology but by reason, that is to say, by an ethical code. The distinction between ideology and interest is a categorical one.

Man does not progress either instinctively or mechanically. He is attracted by exemplary causes, by idealistic goals that are generally proposed by eminent minds. The utopian and human elements that exist in every ideology act as a spur, a factor of social acceleration. In this sense, ideologies fulfill a positively stimulating role. However, the rational mechanisms, that is, the concrete ideas on what is good and what is attainable and the means necessary to achieve it, are administered by ethics and the social sciences. They do so with a greater exactitude and efficiency than "opinion," and without provoking disproportionate tensions. The stimulating function of ideology is so amply surpassed by the tension that it engenders, that in the end such benefits are cancelled out. From this perspective too, the historical assessment of ideologies is unfavorable.

The Dialectics of Ideologies

Our previous discussion was directed principally at established ideologies. There exist also the young, new ones. As they are no more than a compendium of beliefs, they undergo the same process as social uses; they are born, they develop, and they die. The creation of hierarchies according to the models of feudalism and the ancient regime is now an extinct ideology in the West. Instead, nihilism is awakening, and it would be very speculative to predict its destiny. The trajectory of ideologies, like that of humans, is oscillating. Something similar occurs with style, religion, and culture. All describe a curve. But the aesthetic canons persevere, even when they grow old. They vegetate but remain robust and sometimes are reborn and become fashionable again. This does not occur in relation to beliefs, for nothing is more dead than an abandoned dogma. The cycle of cultures does not in any case rigorously correspond to that of ideologies, for several can coexist in the same cultural field. Neither the philosophy of art nor that of culture have solved the problem of the dialectic of ideology. In reality, this seductive field of inquiry has only been obliquely touched upon by the philosophers of history when examining religious movements. Nevertheless, religions and ideologies are governed by rules that, although in part coincident, are essentially disparate.

In spite of the fact that ideologies have millenary precedents, they are relatively modern phenomena. Their great historical flowering coincides with the intervention of the masses in collective life, with the development of the means of communication and with the secularization of knowledge and morality. All this occurred in the second half of the XVIII century. Up to that point, ideologies had a meagre social base and a confused spiritual relationship. The normal pattern of an ideology is as follows. It is born with the appearance of a thesis from a doctrinaire's laboratory: "Man is born free but is everywhere in chains." This conceptual nucleus releases a series of practical consequences, some of which become postulates: "one man, one vote." At a given moment the postulate becomes a general belief: "democracy is the supreme political good." This process is not carried out in a vacuum, but in the midst of contradictions. Tension depends among other factors on the attitude of the political power. If it is adverse, the struggle begins from the bottom up. If it is favorable, then the advance is more rapid, at least externally. If it is neutral, it has to compete with other currents already established or being formed. Sociologically the process is one of growth. But, from the intellectual point of view, it is one of progressive decay. As ideas become mass ideas and are propagated as such, they lose authenticity and truth, and so degenerate.

There comes, however, a moment when the virulence of a given ideology recedes. This is a qualitative as well as a quantitative matter. It concerns decadence, recession and indifference, a lack of militancy and enthusiasm. Those that received authoritarian patronage depend on political situations, and the fall of a protective regime usually means the end of the ideology. This was the case of Nazism. But those that hatch tenaciously confronting the political power last longer and resist decline. As their ascendancy was harder so their decline is slower. It is not therefore exactly true that the collective power follows the ideology of its leader. Rather, governments end up by accepting the predominant ideology. Obviously, this is clear in the demoliberal states, but is also sufficiently true of absolute ones; Paris was, after all, "worth a mass." The decline of an ideology is similar in certain points to that of religion. Its symptoms are the convergence and alliance with other creeds, mutual tolerance and disappearing enthusiasm, the relaxing of spiritual tension and finally the weakening of beliefs, with the consequent formalization of external practice. Schism and war are proofs of ideological vitality. Non-conformity and docility demonstrate the opposite. A coalition of ideologies constitutes suicide. A purely official ideology is something that is socially dead. And so, the symptoms that an observer of present day reality might observe lead him to believe that, as classical religion was extinguished in Rome, so, today, the ideologies that in our time filled the social vacuum of ancient myths, are seeing their own twilight.

III. Political Apathy

The Phenomenon

It is difficult to establish the degree of political awareness in a people. In democracies, its interest in the polity would appear to be manifested through the exercise of the vote. However, electoral absenteeism can sometimes be a political act, while the actual act of voting might be the result of inertia. Moreover, in countries having introduced mandatory voting, the percentages of voters are distorted by the compulsion factor. Statistics must therefore be treated with prudence. The electoral participation in the designation of the U.S. president was 44% in 1920, 49% in 1924, 57% in 1928, 58% in 1932, 61% in 1936, 62% in 1940, 55% in 1944, and 53% in 1943, which amounts to an average of 55%. When the war was over, the percentages declined, particularly in the South, where they rarely reached 20%. There are districts in North America where the participation in local elections oscillates around the 10% mark. In Germany, France and Great Britain participation is somewhat higher.

The abstentionist percentages in Spain are as follows: 35% 1846, 33% 1850, 30% 1851, 38% 1857, 31% 1858, 47% 1865, 30% 1869, 35% 1871, 45% 1872 (54% in the second election), 60% 1873, 45% 1876, 66% (in Madrid) 1879, 29% 1881, 28% 1884, 50% (in Madrid) 1891, 90% (in Barcelona) 1899, 70% 1901, 50% 1903, 75% (in Madrid) 1905, 33% 1907, 46% 1910, 46% 1914 56% 1916, 41% 1918, 48% 1919, 46% 1920, 58% 1923, 30% 1931, 44% 1933. This shows a very high average of non-voters, with a rising trend.

The percentages would be increased if one subtracted the false votes of the traditional gerrymandering. Between 1846 and 1868, 27% of the returning deputies had their credentials contested, more than half of them due to electoral fraud. In 1910, out of the 404 deputies, 139 were re-scrutinized while 119 were elected unopposed. Thus, out of the properly contested seats, only 146 were not the subject of objection. Introducing these correcting factors into the abstentionist percentages we arrive at a figure that is well over half of the electoral census. The participation process therefore follows a descending curve.

Among contemporary states, the Italian is today the one closest to the demo-liberal idea, and is both potentially and theoretically the most open-ended. Any political apathy in this case would be very relevant, as it would occur despite the strong stimulus and permeability of the institutions. The results of the Almond memoranda (Princeton 1962) are highly conclusive: 62% are never interested in political questions, 26% are sometimes, 52% are not interested in political campaigns, 66% never discuss politics, 32% do sometimes, 40% cannot name a single political leader, 73% do not expect their opinions to be taken into consideration by the government, 93% think that they should not actively intervene in local life, 97% are not proud of their political system, 99% do not devote their spare time to civic political activities. And these indices of political apathy in Italy are not exceptional. In France, where the average abstentionism in municipal and legislative elections in the last 15 years (1957-1971) reached 25%, nearly half (47%) of the population declared themselves to be apolitical in a poll made towards the end of 1970, which was, after all, a year of relative tension.

Inhibition on such a considerable scale is not, however, the clearest index of a general climate of political apathy. Much more revealing is this same attitude among the young. In the British election of 1964, out of 3 million new voters, one million had not bothered to register, so a third of the young British citizens had not taken a single step towards the voting urns. The percentages of electoral participation are on the whole either becoming stabilized or decreasing. This occurs in spite of the fact that the West has experienced an intensification and multiplication of social relationships due to the increase of collective activity and the development of the means of mass communication. Moreover, the electoral techniques have been perfected, and access to the voting urns has been made much easier. And in parallel to this, economic progress has strongly increased the cultural level and the political awareness of the citizen. All these factors should have contributed to a growth of electoral participation. But the evidence points to a relatively growing abstentionism.

Political apathy is not solely manifested in suffrage abstentions. There are other symptoms, perhaps less measurable, but still considerably illuminating.

The first is the decrease in party memberships. As trade unions and recreational and technical associations grow, so parties become weaker. There are fewer militants and more indifferent fellow-travelers.

Consequently, the more or less uninterested neutral masses, on whose electoral swing the outcome of an election depends, are growing.

The second symptom is the low level of enthusiasm. Following the fanatical demands made by the totalitarian parties between the wars, the western masses have become increasingly serene. Political rhetoric has suffered a profound mutation; electrifying harangues and mobilizations are no longer fashionable. In their place, we have press conferences and commissions of experts. The politician has abandoned his high-pitched, emphatic frenzy, to model himself on a modest and efficient member of the managerial class. All this is a response to the masses, who have gained in objective critical ability what they have lost in emotional candor. As the cultural level of a society rises, so its emotional outbursts run along channels that are increasingly removed from politics and business. The growing rationalization of human life is relegating enthusiasms to the spheres of art, sport, and emotional intimacy.

The third symptom is the contraction of the genuinely political press. The papers with the greatest circulation are sensationalist, not doctrinaire. The evolution is a very clear one. The old prestige journals that were platforms for an ideology either indulge in popular reporting or become minority organs. The masses are not sufficiently interested in parliamentary debates, electoral promises, and ideological questions. They prefer reading matter far removed from cabinet backchat.

The fourth symptom is that people devote less and less of their increasing leisure time to political questions. Political clubs either transform themselves or cease to exist. The pub conversation has little to do nowadays with matters of government. During weekends and holidays political controversy disappears. It is becoming difficult for parents to share their political anxieties with their children. Fiscal pressure and socialization makes inexorable inroads on inheritances, but the crisis on inherited paternal ideologies is equally great. The Party allegiance of a family disappears not through rebellion, but through lack of adjustment and of interest.

Electoral absenteeism, the decline of party politics and enthusiasm, the demise of the doctrinaire press, the depolitization of leisure time, the dehumanization of the state are at once the causes and the effects of the reduced interest of the citizen for party political action, and for the channeling of his ambitions into other activities. The struggle for power no longer attracts the attention of the average man, as it did half a century ago. But, at the same time, this political apathy constitutes an important testimony to the process of deideologization. The social tensions of the past were generally sustained by ideological fights. The clash between conflicting programs was the greatest motor of polemical and electoral passions. Without doubt the crisis of ideologies is not the only reason for political apathy, and it may not be the most important. Concrete interests also come into play. But it is obvious that the relaxing of collective tensions and the progress of abstentionism coincide with a generalized decline of ideologies.

Assessment

The spatial and temporal scope of the phenomenon has given rise to a controversy which, although more axiological than empirical, is nevertheless of great interest. The question is whether political apathy indicates a good or a bad social order. Those who judge such apathy negatively do so from liberal precepts: an electoral result that contains a strong margin of abstentionism is a caricature of the general will, and the resulting government is a sham. Inhibition substantially falsifies the telling of votes. If it is desirable that people should govern themselves through the exercise of the vote, and that decisions should abide by the majority, an abstention signifies a decision not to collaborate in the common good. One is therefore concerned with the rejection of a duty, an antisocial act that denotes the failure of citizen morality. There is an underlying inclination to see apathy as a pathological social syndrome. This reasoning has been the basis of legislations making voting obligatory. And where such laws have been applied severely, as in Belgium, the results have been satisfactory.

Important objections can be made to such thinking. The exercise of the vote is not a duty, but a right that can be renounced. To abstain is just another way of manifesting an opinion. The compulsion to vote has raised the number of voters, but it has not changed genuine attitudes about the state. Coercion deforms the results because it causes hurried, alienated, and fortuitous reactions; compulsion is antiliberal and humiliating. Man cannot interest himself in the whole spectrum that surrounds him. He can only concentrate successively on certain poles of attention, which presupposes apathy toward others. Therefore, disinterest over politics in general and elections in particular is not an abnormality but an inexorable consequence of the human condition. But the decisive objection is that political apathy, of which electoral absenteeism is a manifestation, is a sign not of malaise but of social health. The statistical studies in the United States show that only a third of those who do not vote abstain because of physical or administrative difficulties. The rest do so out of principle, disinterest, or indifference. Now, a man is only disinterested in a particular question when he views his intervention as useless, or when he thinks that it does not affect him, or affects him less than other matters. One therefore deduces that political apathy is born out of a lack of democratic conviction, a lack of faith in the system, or out of a relative or temporal unconcern with the dialectics of power. In my judgement, the two assumptions have a positive foundation. The first because it shows a tacit acceptance of the rationalization and technification of public life and a disenchantment with public life. The second because it reveals that political conflicts do not constitute real problems. In the developed countries such conscious attitude indicates a degree of personal comfort and loyalty to the structures of authority; an approval of the general course of events. One of the primary causes of social tension is dissatisfaction and unease; it is not surprising that the greatest electoral participation in Democratic Germany was registered on the eve of the National Socialist triumph, and the greatest participation in North America corresponds to the outbreak of World War II. When the system is functioning normally the citizen calms down. But when something menaces his tranquility, he shows his uneasiness and agitation through demonstrations, strikes and the exercise of the vote. By establishing obligatory suffrage, a relatively revealing reference for societies that are civically mature and administratively normal is discarded. In other circumstances the vote might well be the least relevant of facts in determining effective social tension. This is the case in underdeveloped countries, in dictatorships and in exceptional circumstances. In my judgement, as there is more consensus and wellbeing, so there is more accord and confidence. Hence, the health of a free state can be gauged by the degree of its political apathy. The phenomenon is not at all disturbing, rather the opposite.

The Nihilistic Outbreak

One of the phenomena that has lately attracted the attention of politicians, pedagogues and sociologists is the so called youth revolt. Could this evidence be a sign of ideologization and a warning of ideological reactivation in the future? The issue seems to deny the panorama of growing political apathy that has been described. This is a complex matter that cannot be easily understood in a political sense unless it is previously defined at an abstract level.

First, the revolt has not involved youth in general, but just students. In other words, its protagonists are students, particularly those in higher grades. It cannot therefore be characterized as a generational conflict, given the absence of young peasants and workers from the conflict, and not out of lack of information and opportunity, as the case of France has shown.

Secondly, the student element converts the phenomenon into a socially restricted one, as the higher strata of learning represent, even in the most developed countries, a small proportion of the population. Moreover, within the centers of learning themselves, the protestors are in their turn a fraction, of varying importance according to the particular case, but always a minority. It is not therefore a class movement, but one of a group, or more exactly an elite.

Thirdly, the student revolt has some outside support which consists of certain more or less reputable academics and certain political leaders. This is why, according to the time and place, some student demonstrations appear to be part of an ideology or a party. An example of the first is the passing connection of the protest movement with the doctrines of H. Marcuse, or the so-called "new left", with organizations such as Maoism. And with this we arrive at the substantial part, the content of the protest.

Fourthly, a comparative analysis of the events shows a great diversity of objectives. In Portugal it appears that what was demanded was a regime of inorganic democracy. But this cannot be the inspiration behind the Italian students, since theirs is the standard demoliberal state. The French demonstrations were said to have been caused by the desire for University autonomy, but this cannot apply to the Swedish students, since they were already administering their institutions. In England and the United States, more than a student protest, there has been a repudiation of capitalist society, and yet, it is difficult to say that such a repudiation moves the Czech and Hungarian students. We must therefore conclude that, on the international level, there is not a general demand for pedagogic reform, nor an accepted political ideology that might serve as a common denominator of the student movement. There is not a united front of positive demands. It would therefore seem on hindsight that these agitations are instead pretexts for action of another kind, symptoms of something more profound.

Fifthly, there is more than just a variety of admitted derivations and objectives. There are manifest contradictions, which appear when comparing student rebellions in different countries and universities. At the center of many of the rebellions we find the inescapable paradox caused by the simultaneous allegiance to liberalism and socialism. It has been frequent in Spain and in other countries for the same students to demand absolute political liberty, parties, parliamentary life, private initiative and competitiveness, and full socialization, nationalization of the means of production, planned economy, rationalization of individual choice of field, bureaucratization of services, generalized social security, removal of wage differentials. This double commitment to Marx and Rousseau forms more than just a hybrid; in all objectivity it is a *"contradictio in terminis."* The sum of the two systems comes to nothing.

Sixthly, beneath the profuse pluralism and even notorious incoherence of the positive demands, there is a coincidence in the negative objectives. The general protest cannot be reduced to a "yes", but it can be to a "no". The repudiation of authority, be it on a personal or institutional level, is a universal factor in the revolt. The contemporaneous social structures are all rejected. This general threat of liquidation respects neither religious beliefs, moral norms, political institutions, aesthetic criteria, traditions, nor fashions. The opposition to all that exists is complete.

This analysis of the phenomenon coincides with two of its most widespread slogans, which are self-defining: "It is forbidden to forbid" and "all progress immobilizes." The question is whether there is a revival of old tendencies such as anarchism, revolutionarism and skepticism. All three are certainly present, but I believe that the concept that most closely explains the significance of the student revolt is nihilism.

Every idea has its history. It was Ivan Turgenev who, in *Fathers and Sons* (1860) described for the first time as a nihilist a type of young man who had begun to appear in Russian society. It concerned a University student whose doctrinal sources included Rousseau, Hegel, Buchner and Feuerbach. Let us quickly examine the leading thinkers of nihilism. Alexander Herzen (1812-1870) wrote in *After the Tempest* (1850): "long life to chaos and destruction! . . . on passing from the old to the new world everything must be left behind, nothing can be taken. . . There is a marvelous likeness between terror and dialectics." Dimitri Pisarev (1840-1868) wrote "everything that can be destroyed must be destroyed." Sergei Netchaief's *Chatecism* (1847-1882), written in collaboration with the exiled Bakunin, recommended that "night and day we must concern ourselves with one thought alone. The inflexible determination to destroy. We recognize no activity except that of extermination." The nihilist profile existed in Russian literature as well as in politics. Alongside those of Turgenev, there are a series of novels portraying the nihilist. Herzen's *Whose is the fault*, Chernyshevsky's *What is to be done?* Pisensky's *Rough sea*, and several by Dostoyevsky. In them we can trace a human type who rejects the cannons of his time and who extends his rebellion to the length of his hair and the appearance of his clothes. He and his companions in subversion are nonetheless unable to outline a program. Nihilism is not an ideology, it is an antiideology that practically exhausts itself of its own volition. And this is why, in spite of certain superficial parallels, the Marxist Leninist scholarship has refused to recognize the nihilists as genuine precursors. This is also why there is a confusion between the actual content of nihilism and the disparity of interpretations to which some of its most representative figures, Herzen among them, have been subjected.

The present student revolt is not simple neoromanticism. It takes from the romantics the protest, the audacity, the rationalism, the impetus, and theatricality. But it lacks the affirmative unity achieved by this movement in ascetics and politics. Instead, there are numerous points of contact between the University rebellion and Russian nihilism. Their protagonists are a student minority of a bourgeois background that are out of touch with the power structure and the masses. The lack of solidarity with society is shown in dress and in habits. Doctrinally the students are disparate, the systems to which they appeal are contradictory, and coincidences, if any, occur in what is negative. We face a neonihilism in a phase of gestation. That this should occur at the moment of the twilight of ideologies is not surprising. These students without a program are tacit witnesses and involuntary agents of deideologization.

IV: The Convergence of Ideologies

Another clear manifestation of the crisis of ideologies is the symptom of their convergence. When two opposing ideas approach each other, with or without synthesis, they are on the path to extinction. This phenomenon must not be confused with temporal coalitions that exist in order to obtain a greater parliamentary majority, and involves only an occasional and tactical concession, not an irreversible doctrinal evolution. The individual parties within the coalition retain their programs, and when the opportunistic association dissolves itself, the parties return to their original stand. The convergence phenomena of the contemporary political scene concern the very permanent instances of cross breeding, such as those between socialist and radicals or between conservatives and liberals. These are unifying movements between groups that are relatively close politically, yet separated by mostly circumstantial discrepancies. Far more spectacular has been the integrating tendency appeared above all in the West during the last few decades between positions traditionally so incompatible as liberalism and socialism. Although the respective degrees of convergence may be uneven, the process is always a double one. Marxism is becoming more bourgeois, and liberalism is socializing itself.

Socialism Veers Right

The word "socialism" appeared abandoned among the pages of an obscure Parisian revue on a winter's day in 1831, and from this modest birth it mounted the Olympus of utopists. By mid-century the ponderous mind of a German Jew attempted to give the newly born tendency a level of scientific knowledge and world conception. Soon there came the executors, the associations, the parties, which in spite of their structural crises and programmatic hesitations, assumed with anger and without pause the defense of the dispossessed. This complex movement, in which there was fantasy, theory and passion, hammered untiringly for a century and a half on the political conscience of Europe, and contributed decisively to the transformation of capitalist society. This was its positive balance, against a dark negative background of violence and resentment.

There are three elements in Socialism: a social idea, a theoretical foundation, and certain administrative techniques. Philanthropic precursors were followed by systematic doctrinaires, in turn succeeded by political experts. Fourier represented the utopian phase, Marx the scientific one, and Stalin the third, that of power. But these different ingredients, even when examined in isolation, remain difficult to grasp because the objectives, the ideological foundations and the implementations of socialism have undergone sometimes profound variation. The absence of a unifying tradition makes the search for common denominators imperative. Only then can the complex and dynamic socialist phenomena be schematically presented. The most invariable of the socialist ideals is egalitarianism, that is, the repudiation of privileges and major class distinction, the redistribution of capital and income, the identity of opportunities, the suppression of misery, and common good and security. The most permanent base of the heterogeneous social doctrine is Marxism. All previous discoveries are synthesized in it, and what follows from it are more or less orthodox developments. As Halevy remarked: "The History of socialism ends with *The Capital.*" No less confusing is the problem of methods and concrete formulae. The *modi operandi* have been so disparate that they have caused two separate developments, the rightist, Fabian, revisionist tradition, and the leftist or dogmatic, Jacobin one: those of Leninism and living communisms. The split was inconceivable to Marx, who saw socialism simply as a stage towards communism. In spite of it, there is a fundamental shared technique: the nationalization of the means of production as a condition for reaching the egalitarian goal.

Pursuing this analysis, we find that, by the second half of the 20th century, the socialist ideals of social justice have been incorporated into the programs of all the great countries, and that Marxism, convicted before humanity of great crimes, has been doctrinally overcome. The definitive condemnation was made by Keynes, the founder of a new economic theory, when he declared *The Capital* to be "an antiquated economic manual which, in addition to being scientifically in error, lacks interest and is inapplicable to the modern world." As for the techniques, full employment, social security, universal education, and social fiscal policy, have become the common property of all parties. The only major outstanding demand, since the totalitarian recourses of communism have been rejected, is the nationalization of the means of production. This formula, which preceded Marx himself, has come to be the universal electoral slogan of socialism. The Germans adopted it in their programs of Gotha (1875), Erfurt (1891), Heidelberg (1925) and Dortmund (1957). The French socialist party adopted it at its constituent declaration of April 25, 1905. And still at the 1957 British Labor Party congress at Brighton, the motion *Industry Society* approved was a veritable anthology of the reasons for nationalizing. The growing unpopularity of the nationalizing experiment however caused a certain uneasiness over this one remaining vindication. The soviet experience, partially rectified, provoked the crisis of 1921-22 and that of 1932-33 (15 million died of privation according to Falcionelli's *History of Soviet Russia*) and caused the generalization of terror. The Swedish program was very limited, for it left not only agriculture, commerce, and small industry to private initiative, but also omitted to nationalize large industry, with the exception of steel, electricity, and the processing of slate and peat. The French phase, effected in part as a punishment against *collaborationists*, was reduced to electricity, gas, coal, railways, airlines and five banking and insurance institutions; other primary industries such as steel and petrol were left in private hands. The British labor party's first venture into nationalization alienated it from popular favor. Their conservative successors had to return the steel and road transport industries to private initiative. The Trade Unions themselves asked for the nationalization program to be interrupted in 1953. In a Gallup poll in February 1958, 87% of the British electorate declared themselves opposed to the policy of nationalization.

In this largely unfavorable climate, characterized by the almost universal malaise of socialism, the British labor party, the most active doctrinally, reelaborated its program in 1958 in two substantial and carefully thought out pamphlets. The more general one was *The Future Labor Offers You*. Perhaps only to be consequential with itself on the fundamental question of nationalization, it proposed the return to state hands of the steel and road transport industries. On this point, it announced rather timidly that, after a careful and complete study, "those companies that fail on the national scale will be nationalized." The "Expropriation of expropriators" proposed by Marx was therefore reduced to that. In the booklet *Plan For Progress*, it was stated that any planning undertaken "should not be understood as a return to stringent controls," and that there is "no single type of control that is a panacea for all our problems." Moreover, there is not only a promise to stimulate such a capitalist thing as competitiveness; there is also the assertion that all nationalized industries "serve to stimulate cooperation, to avert the choking of production, to test new products, and to promote economic expansion where private initiative proves insufficient." Such texts can be seen as spontaneous rectifications or as tactical retreats caused by hostile public opinion. In either case it means a shift in the position of the Labor party that brings it extraordinarily close to that of the conservatives. A theoretical antecedent of this almost Copernican volte-face that severs socialism from its last remaining classical demand is Anthony Crosland's *The future of socialism* (1957). This book, considered to be one of the most significant on socialist thought to appear in the last quarter of the 20th century, concludes, "It is clear that the ownership of the means of production has ceased to be the key to our society's character. Collectivism, just as much as private ownership of the means of production, is compatible with different degrees of liberty, democracy, equality, worker exploitation, class consciousness, planning, control and economic prosperity." This analysis, illustrated by a convincing parallel between the United States and the Soviet Union, negates one of the most radical hypotheses of Marxism, and one of the most characteristic elements of socialism as it had been understood in the West.

The last word on the labor party came from Harold Wilson in his book, *Purpose on Politics* (1964). Far from rectifying Crosland's line, he pursues it to its ultimate conclusions, emphasizing the deideologization of the party. The most recurring word is realism, and all is based on the fundamental assumption that, in politics as much as in science and technology, amateurs must be disposed of, and it must be recognized that on all levels a prepared and professional mind is required. The methods are extremely flexible; "We must not be dogmatic and doctrinaire about new industries." writes Wilson, "Some will be privately, and others publicly owned." The goals that Wilson outlines are: 1. to produce more scientists; 2. to keep them in the country; 3. to use them more intelligently than in the past; and 4. to organize British industry so that the results of scientific research are applied to the growth of the national income. In the upshot, what labor proposes is to destroy ideological prejudices and to make the administration into a center for scientific research and application. It is pure rationalism and empiricism under the aegis of the experts. It does not really matter if in practice these objectives are hindered by the considerable inertia of Marxist doctrinarism. What is important is that, although the residues of the old labor ideology continue to run along their well-worn paths, there is now a new inspiration at large that draws upon the sciences of state and of society.

The British experience has its counterpart in the program that was approved by the German socialist party, the SPD, at its congress of Bad-Godesberg towards the end of 1959. The project was the work of Ollenhauer, of the economist Deist and of the two most eminent theoreticians of the party, Eichler and Kautsky. It was no improvised novelty; it was a profound revision of the draft project that had been submitted to the congress of Stuttgart in 1958. Published in a 23 page pamphlet, the program consists of an even sharper twist towards economic liberalism and political conservatism than previously undertaken by the British labor movement. Ever since Marx convened the workers of the

World in 1848, socialism had always defined itself everywhere, and particularly in Germany, as the party of the working class. The program of Heidelberg in 1925 was drafted, as the preceding ones, in the name of the workers, die *Arbeiterklasse*. The terminology was maintained in the program of Dortmund of 1952, which is still formally operative. But at that point the SDP abandoned for the first time its working-class identity. The formula employed makes this only too clear: "The German Socialist Party has ceased to be a class party in order to transform into a party of the people." Does this mean that German socialism has generously renounced the class-based resentment that had been its main inspiration for a whole century? No. It means that, contrary to Marx's prophecies, capitalism has not impoverished the masses for the benefit of a few monopolists. Instead, it has in some countries drawn the proletariat into the bourgeoisie by multiplying their riches. The number of dispossessed is consequently reduced, and it is no longer possible in Germany to base a party on their resentment and material needs, while still retaining serious pretensions to gain power in the parliamentary system. In conclusion, German socialism has seen capitalism emancipate its erstwhile clients, and has now been forced to appeal to everybody, in the manner of other parties that do not have class alignments.

Such a turnabout in the sociological composition of the party has its inevitable doctrinal parallel. The SPD has not only repudiated absolutely and for the first time the venerable name of Marx, but has also confessed itself to be "tied to the Christian ethic in traditional humanism and philosophy." It proclaims liberty to be the supreme social value and desires dialogue with other parties on an equal basis. The essential points of classical socialism, dialectical materialism, atheism, authoritarian planning, and the dictatorship of the proletariat are therefore renounced. But the most surprising transformation concerns the economic policies. These are the kernel of any contemporary program, particularly in that of a socialist movement that responds to a material understanding of politics. The volte-face on is so confounding that the more discerning reader will feel a need to verify the translation of the texts, so unlikely do they seem. "The liberty of consumption, of work and of business initiatives are fundamental, and free competitiveness is an important element in all free economies. The autonomy of employer and employee unions in order to agree on tariffs is an essential part of a free political order. Totalitarian economic pressure destroys liberty. Therefore, the SPD proposes a free economy in which agreement is possible." With this declaration of principle, German Socialism rejects one of its basic postulates. For as stated in Von Mises' standard work, "Socialism is a system that admits neither markets, nor prices nor competitiveness." The SPD however goes beyond this. Its apostasy, as far as Marxism is concerned, is almost complete, because its new thesis is the exact opposite of what socialists have preached since the times of Owen. "Private ownership of the means of production is entitled to society's protection." Nationalizations are justified in exceptional circumstances in order to maintain a free market. "Public companies are a decisive means to stimulate production and hinder monopolies." It adds moreover that, in order to avoid any dangerous concentration of economic power in the hands of the State, "Public property has to be decentralized and its administration must be autonomous." We are therefore witnessing the volatilization of socialism's major unfulfilled demand: nationalization. With the rejection of collectivism, thought to be the necessary means to achieve social justice, the last great differentiating feature of socialism as an economic theory distinct from capitalism is abandoned. The importance of the change within the SDP is magnified by the fact that it was one of the most rigidly dogmatic parties of our time. Of its former exceptional doctrinal vigor and progressiveness, hardly anything socialist remains beyond the name. We are accordingly faced with a nominal and declining socialism, that has abandoned its dogma, and is weakened by the loss of almost all its Marxist life-blood.

In western democracies, it is undeniable that socialism is increasingly less of an antithesis and more of a spare part in the party game, an element of relief in the process of government exhaustion. Notwithstanding this, Communism subsists as the purest and most extreme form of Marxism. The homogenization of western politics does not seem to have expanded worldwide. One then wonders whether the convergence of ideologies is just a local phenomenon? Between the two blocks separated by the Iron Curtain there is evidently a doctrinal conflict that has provided fuel to the cold war. But if the international situation is examined closely, it is apparent that, even on the global scale, there are signs of convergence. Ever since World War II we have lived in considerable social tension; Korea, Suez, Quemoy, Hungary, Berlin, the U2 incident, Laos, Cuba, etc., mark the highest points on the international temperature graph. The struggle has been waged with three weapons that, according to Aron, characterize the cold war: dissuasion by threats, persuasion by propaganda, and subversion, that is already violent and constitutes the prelude to a revolutionary war. Occasionally the cold war becomes very hot at local levels; from the 42nd parallel to the Caribbean, passing through the Berlin wall, examples of these abound. Between 1945 and 1962 the day to day life of the statesman has been marked by anguished uncertainly, preparation for the worst, and uninterrupted vigilance. But on the 5th of August 1963 came the unexpected, when the US and the USSR agreed to the suspension of nuclear testing. In spite of its internal limitations and its uncertain historical viability, this document marks the greatest relaxation of international tension during the post-war years. Unfortunately, it has not exactly guaranteed an era of peace. But taking into consideration the relative nature of sociological concepts, it can be said that never since 1945 have men been closer to peace.

The international *détente* is in great part the result of an evolution of communism. The growing economic development of the soviet people is turning the Marxist ideology into something that increasingly resembles an official religion. Russian agriculture no longer responds to extreme collectivism. Instead of egalitarianism, new classes have been created, perhaps with more justification and less separated among themselves than the tsarist, but present and extensive nonetheless. And among all, the Marxist precept of the necessity of war as a means of proletarization has taken refuge in China. The Sino-Soviet split revealed a heresy: A USSR that denied a central dogma. This grave heresy marks the beginning of the disintegration of Marxist ideology within the Soviet block. In Yalta the allies treated the USSR as just another Occidental power. It was a naive and premature gesture which exacted a high and tragic price in Europe. But today the circumstances have greatly changed. The soviet proletariat is becoming more bourgeois and losing its inferiority complex. The center point of the socioeconomic relation between the two blocks is becoming closer and deeper. Marxism is becoming softer. In short, Russia, without abandoning its still rather elemental imperialism, is becoming westernized. And this shift so evidently manifested indicates clearly that ideologies are also converging on an almost planetary scale.

Liberalism Veers Left

The fascinating myth of liberty has presided over the greater part of western political life since the end of an uneasy 18th century. Consciences thrilled to the Jacobin impetus. It was a kind of general delirium, a great popular passion. At few times in history have men been so extensively and so intensely moved by a utopia: individual and collective self-determination, that is, each man free and master of himself, and government for the people by the people. It was the response to the estates system of privilege, and to the divine right of kings that had characterized the ancient regime. This double revolutionary ideal was made juridically concrete in a catalog of the fundamental rights of man, the Declaration of 1789, and in a form of state -a democracy-. One and the other were closely connected because it was thought that only through the exercise of political liberty, that is through a democracy, could juridical liberty, that is the fundamental rights, be guaranteed, and vice versa.

The two ideological pivots of demoliberalism have for a quarter of a century been moving towards areas that are less propitious for the free coexistence of the citizens and for the preponderance of the popular will. There is a slow but palpable approximation to authoritarianism and socialization. The myths are effectively changing; from liberty to security and from representation to fiscalization. The demoliberal ideology, in moving left, is drawing close to its classical rival. At a hypothetical point, neoliberalism and neosocialism meet.

Liberty is, to be sure, a desirable good. It admits no limits on the essential level. But on the plane of actual existence, all human behavior finds itself flanked by "duty" and "power". Namely, by moral imperatives and historical possibilities. But this is not a static situation. In our time judicial norms and the conditions of life effectively reduce the possibilities of selfdetermination. The liberal principle of individual sovereignty, as it gives way to the demands of reality, becomes increasingly abstract.

Analyzing the phenomenon factually one starts with man's two types of activity. The first is leisure, which is diverting, and the second is work, which is necessary. For millennia, work and self-defense have occupied the immense majority of man's waking hours. The inflexion point is contemporary. General security has overcome the anguish of personal safety. The diminution of the active working day has increased the amount of free time. It is not that we are moving towards a paradise or towards an inferno of *Dolce far niente*; we are moving towards a general raising of the standards of living that will allow all to enjoy the benefits of leisure, once enjoyed solely by the bourgeoisie. The question is whether this relative manumission of a biblical sentence increases the possibilities of actual selfdetermination. If this is confined to the working day the answer is no. The diminution of the working day corresponds to an increase in productivity, which in turn requires greater specialization and focus: a qualitative concentration of effort. Work will therefore be increasingly purified of distractions and pauses. It will be totally absorbing, and one will enter its orbit with the implacable servitude of a satellite.

The empirical analysis of leisure meanwhile produces unexpected results. That the average North American works 37 hours a week does not mean that the remaining 131 hours may be devoted to some sort of hobby. Out of those hours must come his normal rest time, and an additional period of relaxation to ease the nervous tension caused by the immense effort and responsibility that the technical age demands. Further consumers of leisure time are the domestic and household tasks, which grow as the service class disappears, and all the social promise and obligations that are part of a public relations syndrome. Finally, there are all the secondary jobs and overtime hours that are by no means the monopoly of poor countries. In the countries boasting a higher per capita income, the process of emulation and propaganda drags man irresistibly towards greater consumption. What is left is leisure time proper, but experience shows that it is becoming subject to increasingly stereotyped regulations. Leisure, like work, tends to accumulate at certain periods that are common to everyone: the weekend and the vacations. This chronological coincidence creates grave problems of overcrowding, which in turn need rationalization and limitations; it becomes more and more difficult to find a place in a train or a space to seat on a beach. The use of free time has now got to be planned in the same way as work might be, and the actual element of choice, as the travel agencies and leisure organizations well know, is really rather small. It is one thing for leisure to free man from his work, and quite another for leisure to increase the limits of man's self-determination. The civilization *des loisirs* involves both an increase in leisure activities and their social organization. It is not impossible that a day will come when each citizen will be allotted a time and a place in the countryside or by the sea when and where he is allowed to go. The increase of leisure time does not alter the tendency of an increasingly rationalized society to reduce the possibilities of self-determination and improvisation.

A judicial situation corresponds to this state of affairs. The modern state forced the rationalization of tolerance which implies the mobilization, organization, and specialization of all human resources. It is a kind of general bureaucratization that can ultimately take the form of a military discipline. This interventionism corresponds to a disappearance of the liberal professions, which gain in stable security what they lose in independence. The result is that the citizen becomes a gear in a large machine that gains in complexity, magnitude, and precision. The margins of discretion in an individual shrink, and with them the possibilities of actual self-determination. The greater the individual's involvement in the system, the fewer his practical rights. The absence of risks implies the absence of options to choose from.

What distinguishes an advanced society from a primitive one is that the first has many more prohibitions and regulations. The present sphere of individual sovereignty is fixed by what others are not able to do, rather than by what one is actually able to do oneself. Liberty is negatively expressed. The situation is reflected in any judicial situation, but particularly in those involving possessions. 19th century liberalism still understood property in the roman manner, as the right to use and abuse one's possessions. Today, property is conditioned by its social character, and any abuse of it is proscribed. Nor is one now free to demand, pay, transfer, and dispose of it as one would wish. The anti-monopoly laws, the organization of investment, the subsidies to agriculture and exports, the protected industries, the minimum wage, the graduated taxation, the maximum earnings, the public companies, the state economic plans are just some within the interminable list of limitations that today's citizen has to endure.

The profound evolution of liberalism is most apparent in economic matters. The physiocratic dogma of *laissez-faire* and the belief in an invisible hand and natural laws that automatically regulate and balance the market are gone forever. Since 1926, when Keynes published *The end of Laissez-faire*, pure economic liberalism has remained theoretically untenable. Its most obvious deficiencies include the imbalance between savings and investment, the unequal distribution of income, monopolies and redundancy, and insecurity in labor. In order to stimulate the complete use of capital and full employment, to establish social security, to maintain competition and to avoid the great differences in the distribution of the national income, certain state controls are imposed. There are interventionist correctives to proper economic liberalism. It certainly does not involve complete Marxist planning and collectivization, but it is a compromise between private ownership of the means of production and the free action of supply and demand on the one hand and the necessities of social justice on the other. This formula is known as neoliberalism or the social regimentation of the market, and it is the order of the day in the West. Pure economic liberalism has passed into history.

But it is not only because of factual and juridical-political causes that the exercise of concrete liberty is becoming difficult; the very myth of liberty is on the wane. The mass is more interested in security, and attempts to suppress such romantic notions as risk and adventure. The goal is to know when to stop. It is virtually economic and judicial determinism. There is an inverse relation between being safe and being free. The castle wall eliminates danger, but it also limits one's horizons. A promotion ladder gives everyone guarantees, but it also classifies all. By making a square formation the rearguard is safe; but mobility is lost. The political price of security is a set of regulations that extend themselves into the future. In short, the spirit of independence, of sovereignty, of spontaneity and of initiative that liberalism had inculcated in individuals is decidedly mutilated.

A similar process occurs over representation. The demoliberal format has the appearance of an equation. Each citizen has an equal vote, the majority decides, the representative organ of a popular will is a chamber elected by inorganic universal suffrage, and this chamber maintains confidence in or withdraws it from the cabinet. In this way the ideal that people should govern themselves was hopefully to be maintained. But in fact, as Rousseau recognized, the *general will* is irrepresentable. Today the whole world knows or feels that between the vote deposited in the urn and the legislation that is promulgated, so many arbitrary mechanisms are interposed, that it is as if the electorate had never existed. Moreover, even in those countries with universal female suffrage, those below a certain age do not vote. A second mechanism is the establishment of electoral boundaries; the transference of her district can swing a majority from one direction to another. Then there is the actual selection of candidates, a task of tremendous importance in which the people do not intervene. A fourth device is a system of telling the votes, which in itself can determine the final results. This was shown in the first general elections of the fifth Republic in France, where the majority vote after two rounds gave 10 seats to the communists and 189 to the Gaullist. But had the electoral system been of integral proportional representation, the communists would have gained 88 seats and the Gaullists only 82. One may add to this list the falsification and corruption of electoral records and procedures. Party discipline, which impedes deputies from voting according to the wishes of their constituents or the dictate or individual conscience, is a further arbitrary device, as is the predominance of commissions of experts on draft legislation. Finally, there is the curtailment of parliament's legislative faculties by the government on the usually very well founded grounds of avoiding any interruption in public business. One wonders whether with so much manipulation there is any part of a legislation which really represents the electorate. But that is not the end of it. When there are many parties, the chamber is so split that the norm is a coalition government, constantly threatened by real or tactical dissidence. Government instability has reached unprecedented heights. The constitution of the French fourth republic, approved in 1946 by only a third of the electorate, was the archetypal example of demoliberal purity. During the period of its embarrassing existence, between December 1946 and May 1958, 23 governments succeeded each other with an average duration of 6 months. Some of them did not last one week. Something similar happened in the second Spanish Republic: Between April 1931 and July 1936, 17 cabinets were formed which lasted for an average of only 112 days each.

The demoliberal program of representation appears to be a fiction. But neither does a straight line exist in nature, notwithstanding which, Euclid's geometry has been largely instrumental for the technical progress of humanity. The worst of it is that the program, either has to be falsified, or causes instability. The strengthening and continuity of the state is indispensable to guarantee the collective security to which we all aspire. This does not mean that representation is to disappear and that there will be a return to the absolutist millennium. Authority is certainly much sought after, but what is most important, more crucial even than being represented by the government, is to be able to control the public activity in order to impede its excesses and cooperate in its efficiency. For this reason, the liberty of expression, and the right of appeal and litigation are already more important than the exercise of the vote. Popular opinions polls lend dignity to simple referenda and wrest it from the more complicated formulae of proportional elections: Such a measure of appeal to popular opinion is in practice a strict measure of control, an open channel for censure. What is really decided is the degree of credibility and confidence rather than any specific question. The inescapable failure of totalitarian communism is that it proscribes all possibilities of genuine control and censure.

In conclusion liberalism is declining. Its two foundational stones are crumbling, in part because they are unrealizable, but also because they are not practical. In the recorded scale of existing values, security and control are more important than liberty and representation. This readjustment brings liberalism closer to socialism.

We have attempted to show that neoliberalism and neosocialism are converging, and that ideologies are becoming less utopian and less virulent.

Cosmopolitanism

Cosmopolitanism, once a minority attitude, gains new adepts every day. The unifying continental movements have become so important that they cannot be ignored in today's international politics, nor when planning future policies. The world is regrouping, not just in relatively circumstantial blocks, but also in higher units. Americanism and Europeism have begun to form new institutions, though of different caliber in each case. Nationalism is declining in the West, and the increasingly rare appeals to it are every day more timid. The occasional brilliant exception tainted with nostalgia confirms the rule. And over and above the federating currents, there is an authentic cosmopolitanism, still in the embryo stage, but nevertheless amounting to a clear and insistent demand for supranational justice. This reality acquires its full meaning within the context of the twilight of ideologies because it is part of the same process. Nationalisms, although not strictly speaking ideologies, tend to function as such. Their fundamental basis is certainly far more emotive than deductive. In contrast, cosmopolitanism is on the one hand a rationalist attitude, and, on the other, a way of integrating and overcoming national particularisms. As such, it is a manifestation of the convergence, and hence, of the decline of ideologies.

It is a historical fact that cosmopolitanism has philosophic origins. It was one of the defining characteristics of the oriental and the Hellenistic wisdoms. It occurs in the oldest speculative tradition, that of Yu in the 3rd. millennium before Christ. He declared, as later echoed by Confucius and his school, "All men that live within the four seas are brothers." (Lun-Yu, IX,13). The Greek stoics, the heirs of Asian wisdom, liked to call themselves citizens of the world. Zeno of Citium considered that "All people form one sole flock." (Frag.262). Epictetus distinguished between "Great and small citizenships" (Diatr.,15,6,10), between the universe and the city. The Latins maintained the tradition. "We are co-citizens," wrote Marcus Aurelius, "We form part of a common political body, and the world is like a city." (Thoughts 4,4,1). And Seneca declared "We are born to live together, our society is like a cavern whose roof would collapse if we did not mutually sustain it" (Ep.Luc.95). Philosophers, not poets outlined cosmopolitanism, and, in the West, they also postulated impassivity, self-control and a life ordered by reason. It was logical that cosmopolitanism, being a reflective and intellectual attitude, should be propagated in this manner. The idea that one must always be with the nation, even when it errs or acts criminally, is an extrapolation of filial love; it is a somewhat refined form of iniquity, more precisely, a group egoism. In so far as it is emotional, nationalism is irrational. And it is the more so in the measure in which it arbitrarily restricts the common good to a national group. On the contrary, cosmopolitanism is the fruit of the rationalization of the political conscience, and is consequently a deideologizing factor.

Nationalisms always define themselves by means of a reciprocal contrast. Their history is always comparative and based on oppositional relationships: separatism, imperialism, annexation, autonomy, etc. If nationalities sustain themselves by confronting others, their field of action clearly lies in foreign politics. And diplomacy has been primarily the maieutic of nationalities. Nationalism is a sentimental and polemical affirmation that can be made without any recourse for technical complexities. It has always been a powerful historical motor, even at times of little economic and social development, and with illiterate leaders at the head. Nationalism responds to a primitive mentality and has no need for precision. Cosmopolitanism however, in order to be crystalized into concrete institutions, requires complicated administrative mechanisms and a highly elaborated economic and judicial knowledge. Federalism and in general all the methods of integrating nationalities are among the most difficult and specialized areas of public law. European unity, the most encouraging supranational undertaking of our time is being forged with great precision, as the CECA and the EEC illustrate. The social sciences reach their most esoteric and purified conclusions when they are applied to pan-European institutions. Cosmopolitanism is rationalist not only because of its origins and foundations, but also because of the technical acumen that its realization demands.

From the sociological point of view, cosmopolitanism is an integrating movement that reconciles the interests of a fraction with those of all. It is the substitution of patriotism by the sentiment of universal solidarity, and a sense of belonging to the human race. The common national goods -

bonum civitates-, as they become part of universal goods -*bonum orbis*-, lose their original irreducibility and pugnacity, and end up becoming compatible with each other through a series of concessions and cuts. Cosmopolitanism is ultimately a combination of nationalisms; it could be geometrically represented as a process of convergence into a single focal point. Cosmopolitanism is, even more than the bourgeoisification of socialism, a case of ideological unification, and so, it implies a moderation of social tensions. Cosmopolitanism is therefore a testimony to the rationalization of political attitudes, and, at the same time, to ideological convergence. It is, in sum, a phenomenon fitting perfectly within the crepuscular process, that can be documented from so many perspectives.

V. The Rationalization of Politics

There is no lack of books on the content and method of politics. The disagreement among the political professionals, both in theory and practice over the object of their study, is even greater than that among philosophers. This is not the place to sum up the polemic. We only refer to it in as far as it is necessary to show the process of rationalization that all sciences, but in particular the social sciences, are undergoing. We have to distinguish between three basic meanings: politics as the philosophy of the common good and of public duty, politics as the art of obtaining and exercising power, politics as the science of the behavior of authority structures and of the relationships between the means and the ends of the community.

The Horizon of the Ends

The first meaning is the oldest; nearly all the classical writers conceived politics as an inventory of norms, duties, rules, and ultimate ends. The actual problems were not totally ignored but the principal object was to determine what ought to be. The source of all political precepts was natural law, and the study was conjectural and deductive. A better absolute, a political optimum was sought. The cardinal point of reference was justice. Such a treatment of the problem caused it to be absorbed into morality. If politics is understood in terms of norms and ideals then it becomes part of ethics, and ultimately it becomes a homily. Treatises such as Welty's *Sozialkathechismus* give an approximate idea of the degree of elaborate doctrinarism which social ethics has attained. It is truly a masterpiece of moral obligations. The extremes of rationalization that were achieved within this field by Aristotelian-Thomist philosophy will not easily be surpassed; they are a specialized field, and, in its context, the slogans of certain demagogues appear like a return to the first postulates of Euclid. There is little new ground to discover where ultimate ends are concerned. We must be more modest and enquire and learn from our enquiries.

The framework of an ideal state -a monarchy, an aristocracy, a republic- is usually formed by the enumeration of the fundamental rights, of legislative criteria, and of desirable conditions for collective life. In this case it is not solely a question of proclaiming the ends but also of proposing the means to achieve them. However, on this point there is a further essential difference between utopian and sociological thought. When Plato postulates a philosopher king, or when Marx preaches the dictatorship of the proletariat, they are referring to institutions that are instrumental in realizing the common good. They have not chosen them a posteriori, that is, after establishing a relationship of cause and effect, as a sociologist might do when he recommends a majority suffrage in order to reduce the number of political parties. The reasoning of the political philosopher is of another kind. For example, division in a city is a social evil, the rule of one man is incompatible with division, therefore monarchy is good. But this way of approaching politics has certain deficiencies. The philosopher is not working with real evidence; he is sifting through possible, simplified, or artificial data. The Platonic *polis* never existed. Moreover, the philosopher disregards the suitability of projected political forms in concrete situations, and ignores their viability. It is often forgotten in this context that a wide margin separates the model state from its historical reality. Moreover, a causal relationship is established by a deductive process from very elementary situations, and allied factors which might have a decisive effect are therefore eliminated. A similar discrimination occurs over the selection of the end on which the government is based: if liberty is preferred, then the goodness of democracy will be deduced, and if it is order, then dictatorship will be praised. It would then appear that all classical arguments over the best form of government, examined out of their context, have always been as entertaining as they have been byzantine.

It is certainly possible to draw conclusions about existing political circles on the basis of the efficiency of their actions. But it is not possible to do this when dealing with the hypothetical products created by thinkers. These may be evaluated on the level of essence according to the precepts of logic and of ethics; but as far as their existence is concerned, they are neutral. To compare monarchy and aristocracy in the abstract is like comparing a saw with a scythe. The extent of the efficiency of each depends on how they developed. That is, on their suitability for specified moments and purposes. In the case of the project for the demoliberal state, in spite of all of its detail and coherence, one is faced with a pure deduction from the postulate "government for the people by the people" which has nothing to do with day to day life. Political philosophy, even under the apparently pragmatic task of specifying the ideal city, remains on the ethical level of what ought to be.

There is rather more realism in the treaties on constitutional law, from the lost one that Aristotle wrote on Hellade to the most exhaustive of the present day, as they describe political forms that have already been promulgated. But in this case too one remains in the normative sphere, since political constitutions do not describe the state, but deal with the way in which the legislators would like it to be. There naturally tends to be a great gulf between the real and the legal state; specifically, in constitutional law one is concerned with ultimate ends. Nevertheless, it is a very useful discipline when it is compared to events, and when the effective functioning of constitutions is studied. But this already amounts to a sociological approach and an empirical understanding of politics.

Whatever the pragmatic limitations of social ethics, political conjecture, and its variant, constitutional law, the three disciplines have reached a degree of rationalization, specialization and esoterism that precludes a generalized approach to them. Political development today, even when politics is taken to be a branch of morality, is moving away from ideological formulae.

Protopolitics and Politics

The actual approach to sovereignty is not a strictly political matter; it is prepolitical, or protopolitical, a primitive approach. We owe to the first major theorist, Machiavelli, a series of precepts, in part intuitive, in part the result of experience, on gaining and maintaining power over the principality. He ignored morality in order to concentrate on the technical aspects. Machiavelli's work lacks system and is even contradictory; it is elementary, disjoined and scarcely useful. Its greatest value lies in its pioneering methodological realism, for the few discoveries it makes may be quickly summed up. Power is obtained through violence and cunning, and is retained through internal and external order. To maintain internal order, it is necessary to establish an equilibrium between the minorities (by intrigue) and social peace (through the police). To maintain external order, it is necessary to use guile (diplomacy) and war (strategy). Of these four arts, Machiavelli only properly developed the last. Perhaps because of this, his recipes have only really been useful to born caudillos. Protopolitics are the result of instinct and intuition. Since the renaissance they have made little progress towards democratic structures. Today a manual for an electoral candidate will have made some practical advance over "The Prince," but it would still be unable to rationalize the technique of gaining power.

Once the first hurdle of protopolitics has been crossed, once power has been obtained, the situation is very different. Limiting the analysis to the modern state, one can observe the disjointed but irreversible quantitative and qualitative growth of public activity. For centuries legislation was nothing more than a commentary and an elaboration of Roman law, education was the concern of the universities and the religious institutions, public works were few and far between, political economy amounted in reality to the budgeting of the royal exchequer, and the administrative and military techniques did not develop. There is an enormous gulf between the renaissance state and the modern one: the quantitative change has been very great. From the sporadic and oral catechism, we have arrived at general obligatory education; from the path, the aqueduct and the forge to motorways, hydroelectric dams and heavy engineering; from mercenary soldiers and fencing to national service and electronics; and from a compilation of the classics, to specialized and technical legislation.

More than 80% of the activity of the modern state concerns the economy: the promotion and execution of economic matters, as well as their ordering and accounting. Economics is a highly elaborate science. It is the study of markets. The creation of wealth is the application of pure science. Just as the doctor substituted the monarch's will in everything that concerned his health, so today the jurists, sociologists, economists, and engineers replace the prince in the majority of the actual government decisions. This means not the birth of a bureaucratic empire, but a further step in the rationalization of the polity. The conquest of power is no longer primarily important; the real political task begins later, attempting to resolve the problems of collective development. Actual government action is increasingly less intuitive and more of a technique; it is a matter for experts and not for amateurs.

If protopolitics represents the zero level of public life, the point at which one begins to govern, the pure politician is something akin to a sociologist's universal. He is present by analogy in all the communitarian order, and in fact this is something very simple. In practice a state needs only two pure politicians: One at the head of the administration and the other exercising control over it. The two should be the visible heads of the government and of the opposition. Obviously, a larger group is needed to recruit them, though a minority one. The pure politician is therefore something that developed communities need in minimal quantities, but which in great doses can bring an explosion of social energy, and its degeneration into personal rivalry over questions of order and procedure.

The Mechanism of the Means

It is an open question whether human behavior, something as concrete and free as man's activities, can be the object of scientific research. The philosophy of history has attempted to give an answer to this problem, which is as old as it is important. Unfortunately, the results have been rather disjointed, and above all, out of proportion, since the field that must be covered includes such vast sets as peoples and civilizations. The scientific treatment of human behavior started with sociology and empirical psychology, both relatively recent disciplines that apply to man the positive methods that were formerly applied to nature. In fact, such methods involve the combination of speculation and observation and, contrary to what was believed for a long time, it is applicable to any form of knowledge. What happens is that, when the study is directed toward human behavior, there is the irrational and individualistic factor of liberty. This causes one to experiment not with an isolated element, as in chemistry, but with great numbers. There is a further major obstacle; it is easy in physics for example to alter a variable such as the temperature. But in sociology one cannot repeat a revolution or invert a war. Nor is it possible in psychology to recreate an experience with protagonists of a different race or sex. To modify one or the other, the subject must be substituted, totally altering the experiment. In spite of this, the positive sciences of man, aided by mathematics, principally statistics, have managed to describe with a great degree of clarity and simplicity such complex phenomena as intellectual stature, personality type, and public opinion. They have also managed to formulate certain laws which, as they are observed with some regularity, allow for forecasts and programming.

Anthropology, like sociology and psychology, is at its beginnings. These are uncertain sciences, as much because of their novelty, as due to the time required to synthesize and to generally cope with the torrent of facts that their experiments disclose. The youngest member in this family of positive sciences is political science, which I consider to be the branch of sociology that concerns the structure of suprafamiliar authority. Its object is neither to streamline ideals, nor to promulgate norms nor to justify desires. It is purely and simply to describe a man's political behavior. It is not a question of setting out what ought to be done, but of knowing what actually happens. What type of ruler do tens of millions of citizens want at any political moment? This can already be answered with a degree of accuracy without any need to turn to questionnaires or referenda. Data of this type is essential for the administration and governing of a society. But the major question involves the means that will lead to a given end. In other words: given such measures, what will happen? This unknown can only be resolved by establishing a law or a functional relationship between certain variables. Political science already has certain propositions of this kind: a) the division of power into executive, judiciary, and legislative renders a dictatorship impossible; b) the number of members of the lower chamber tends to be the cube root of the whole population; c) every political party degenerates into an oligarchical body; d) proportional representation leads to a multiparty system, and a two party system is the result of a winner-take-all on one round of voting; e) a confrontation between a chamber elected by universal suffrage and another composed by members born or designated leads to the annulment of the second.

There is an embryo of positive political science and a hopeful field of development. It is rather surprising that there can still be polemics today on the disadvantages of the multi-party system and the necessity of representing minorities, when the laws set down by Duverger have reduced the problem to an option. Statesmen as much as the masses ignore the fact that, alongside traditional engineering, there is also social engineering, that is, a rational understanding of the relationships of authority, the efficiency of institutions and the behavior of groups. The balance after only a decade give some promise of the extent of its possibilities and perspectives. From now, the method of approximation and guesswork must be abandoned in favor of a degree of exactness. This applies not only to the 80% of the government involving economic science, but also in what concerns the structural framework of authority. Given certain goals, political science will recommend the most suitable means of achieving them. But it will never be possible to provide the actual end. In the same way as physics can be employed for good or for bad, to build or to annihilate, there can always be tyrannies and bad administrations, whatever advances political science may make.

Theoretically its position is subordinate. But economics is also in principle an auxiliary knowledge to the political one. Yet it is ultimately the dominant partner, because the ends of order, justice and material and cultural development are matters that a statesman cannot ignore for fear of destroying himself. These ends are not necessarily realized in a concrete situation by a sovereign decree or a majority vote: their achievement lies in the economic and political sciences. There are innumerable political and administrative problems having only one good solution. That demanded not by ideological party principles, but by physico-mathematical and sociological laws. In spite of their constitutively aseptic and instrumental character, the efficiency of positive knowledge, inserted in the context of given ends, lends it a strongly imperative axiological dimension.

The Expert

Every constitutional form and every change in a community's structure corresponds to a type of governor. The demo-liberal state, consolidated scarcely a century ago, produced a type of politician that was distinct from preceding ones. He was quite different from the medieval lord, the renaissance chancellor, the baroque court favorite, and the 18th century enlightened man. The public figure of the demoliberal state was a rhetorical ideologue, for words prevailed over action, and form over content. His major instrument of government was the spoken word, which he used to cast spells over the multitude, rather than as a framework for true ideas. The rhetorical politician was a man of commonplaces, not of concrete knowledge. He had an agile mind with touches of sophistry. He was a kind of collective trouble seeker. If the roman senators satisfied their people with bread and circus, these politicians did it with great gestures and generalized ideas, utopic illusions, florid declamations, and emotional appeals. This form of government was to an extent licit while there was little progress in the social sciences. It was also perfectly possible while the low cultural level of the masses and their material underdevelopment kept popular demands within modest limits.

But the situation has now changed. Science and action have replaced the spoken word in politics. Politics in no longer a saying; it is a doing, doing *something more*. That *more* can be constitutional law, or social security or economics. The point is that it is a rigorous discipline. Moreover, the people have ceased to be a passive, receptive audience; words are accepted only for a period, after which they must be acted upon. Speeches, programs, declarations of principle, even evident good intentions, are mere celestial music. Concrete achievements, however, do impress. A government justifies itself through its concrete measurable acts, not by its sayings.

Another type of politician -the expert- corresponds to the rationalization of the social sciences and the transformation of the popular mentality and popular demands. His intellectual baggage is science instead of ideology. He depends on actions, not words. His appearance is neither ostentatious nor theatrical but efficient and modest. He is neither an amateur nor an improviser, and represents reason rather than desires. He attains power not through street smartness, but through the sum of his achievements and his capacity for theory and practice. He is the total opposite to the promiscuous dilettantism of the rhetorical ideologue. In large companies, managers are taking the place of general meetings and even board meetings, and for some time now, advisory commissions have replaced ministers and legislative assemblies in certain spheres. The State in short is also becoming functional and technical; it is handing itself over to the experts. This is not an exception, but is rather part of a general process of change that is affecting every level and every area. Human life, not just politics, is achieving previously unknown degrees of rationalization. Auger's extraordinary statistic is already well known: 90% of the scientists and researchers that have existed since the beginning of history are alive today. Or to put it differently, in half a century the logos has extended itself beyond what it had in the previous 100 millennia. How could politics be expected to escape a process of rationalization that, against the background of history, assumes such enormous proportions? Experts have flourished everywhere and, logically, they have also flourished in the state.

Does this herald a period of depolitization, as the opponents of the rationalization process argue? No; it involves a process of deideologization, and a saturation of politics with a more rational content. Moreover, at the highest levels, each expert is part of the government, and, as such, is co-responsible for the nation's direction. Although centered on a specific sector, this particular vision of the common good must be wide and consensual. Specialization in particular areas is compatible with a broad consciousness of the state. Nor in this sense can one refer to apolitical experts in the higher echelons of the different hierarchies. Serious scientific advances and profound social mutations need new modes. To govern is a job that, like one in electronics, is becoming more complicated. From politics as an art and a rhetoric, we are moving towards politics as a science and a technique. It is anachronistic to look upon politics in any other light. As the rhetorical ideologues fade into history, the expert enters the limelight.

The Ideologue

The man who cultivates "ideological though" is not an authentic intellectual. He is simply interested in political power. The unions of such men form pressure groups, not philosophical schools. This can be shown both deductively and experimentally. On the first count an ideology is a popularized political philosophy, and is therefore very far from constituting scientific thought. The greatest fault for what Spengler called the homo *theoreticus* is to be ideological, which must be avoided as the devil. The man who is practical, yet wishes to cloak his desires as thought, finds the ideal way out in ideologies. He can affect reflection and neutral speculation while remaining actively egotistical and committed. One does not arrive at an ideology as one might arrive at a theorem, because it is a pleasure to discover a truth, no matter how unpractical. An ideology is not a happy find, but an instrument forged for the purpose of mobilizing the masses. Whatever the social panacea that he might flourish, every ideologue is moved by a passion to command.

Historical experience ratifies this analysis. There are those, Tiberius and Cesar Borgia are the most notorious, who sought naked power and sovereignty without any pretense at justification. There are also citizens who, without seeking it, and almost despite of themselves, are promoted to the leadership of the state by grace and virtue of society's mechanisms. This shows that there has been an abundance of rulers who did not come from an ideological background, while history does not recall any ideologue who did not desire power. If we examine the spokesmen for liberalism, socialism, fascism, and communism, we find that there is not a single pure theorist among them. They wrote for agitators, not for scholars. Their professed intention is to reach the shop floor and the village pub, and this is even truer in the followers of the ideologues. Ever since the masses began to intervene decisively in public life, that is, ever since the French Revolution, politics has been packed with ideologues, that is, with power seekers, who manipulate pseudo-ideas in order to delight their audiences; and the counterrevolutionary ones are not always an exception.

Do ideologies decline because there is less desire for political power? No, but the twilight of ideologies allows people with a vocation for government to do without them, and to choose other more suitable and contemporary means to conquer power. For over a century the way into politics consisted generally in swearing loyalty to some vague slogans and to the party that represented them. There then started a career that, passing through the various levels of mayor, deputy and undersecretary, finally ended up at a ministerial level. It was not necessary to know anything about finances to head an exchequer, nor about education to head that ministry, nor about economics to be minister of commerce. Politics was an instinctive profession, empirical and full of generalities which made it unnecessary to master a particular discipline. Today things have changed, among other reasons because of the growing complexity of the administration. All over Europe we see people who reach the government straight from the library, the laboratory, the factory, or the professional office, without ever having entered the political career ladder. They reach those posts because they are experts, because they have knowledge and are useful. The same thing that happens in politics happens in industry, research, or any other form of rationalized collective activity.

The remainder of the 20th century bodes ill for the surviving recalcitrant ideologues. All retain hopes of office, but few will achieve it. The ideologues will become bitter and resentful. The most unsettling issue for them is the obvious observation that their presumed theories can be reduced to nothing more than a rampant, avid will for power. On the end, the ideological puppet show will be over, and the tragi-comic person will remain on the stage – a man who has always hidden his desire to govern, and who has had to endure being governed.

Ambition is the motor of progress and there is no cause to censure its licit manifestations, although to me an ambition to rule has always appeared crude and lacking in compensation. What at this stage appears difficult to accept is the pretension to rule without being an expert in any of the knowledges that are required to govern the state. Every genuine intellectual must really convey this, already over-repeated message: an ideologue is not a thinker: he is a candidate for a council post, for a governorship, who sublimates his appetite for power into a mental sub-product that is scarcely valid.

From Power to Authority

The distinction between power and authority can first be found in a disputed passage of Augustus' *Res Gestae*. It never really crystalized completely in either private or public roman law. Thomas Aquinas distinguished between political power (*potestas*) and the capacity for acting or potency (*potentia*). He concluded that "power is a potency with a certain preeminence and authority. Already in this all important text there appears a dangerous confusion between *potestas* and *auctoritas*, which unfortunately all the scholastics were to follow. Francisco de Vitoria is a typical example. "Power," he wrote, "is the authority to govern." Throughout his work he uses *potestas* and *auctoritas* interchangeably. In our days, neo-scholastics, stimulated by sociology, have attempted to counterpose the two notions. "Power," wrote Maritain. "is the force that permits us to pressure others, while authority is the right to command." But this approach rests on morality since it contains an explicit moral judgment: the legitimate authority to power.

The distinction is not just nominal, nor one of terminology. It is essential in its practical consequences. There is no need to base it on norms, as it streams from facts. The distinction can be empirically and phenomenologically based. Political power is held by the man in a situation enabling him to force his will on the individuals of a group. It is accordingly the capacity to order about a free being. Instead, "authority" is the possession to an eminent degree of a recognized virtue. Unlike "prestige," it requires certain real qualities in addition to favorable public opinion.

By its origin, political power is something that is granted outside of itself, while authority is internal and autonomous. No one is naturally powerful; one is powerful only by accident. Dialectically it is a *non sequitur* to claim that sovereignty is received, since it is born of consensus. It is not gained by one alone but is the result of the delegation of the people. Factually things occur in an analogous manner; one is on the throne thanks to the support and loyalty of others, even in the case of the hereditary king or the tyrant. There is no strictly autonomous political power. Political power is deposited, and all legitimacy can be reduced to consent. Instead, authority is born of the very perfectioning of knowledge and practice. The foundations of authority are not to be found in others, but lie in one's own merits. It is neither a legacy nor an accidental condition; it is something that is created, and is the second nature of the "author." One "happens to be" in power, while one "possesses" authority, or more exactly one "is" in it. We alone can rid ourselves of authority. It is essentially autocratic.

By its operational mode, political power is coercive, and even the most democratic requires violence. Its object is human freedom, and its intention is to subjugate it, at least partially and temporarily. The exercise of command has spilled so much blood over the world, that against it, the cruelest activities appear comparatively tame. The old history of sovereignty is inexorably violent; the curial chair and the praetorian guard are as inseparable as the axes and staves borne by the lectors. One cannot order without wounding. Authority in contrast is inoffensive and pacific; it helps us without upsetting us. It consists of advice, not order. And is neither sought nor feared. There is nothing so comforting, so hospitable as the "argument of authority" or its philological translation referred to as "the dictionary of authorities." One consults it to be in good company. One does not increase one's authority by killing. Like Socrates, one confirms it by sacrifice.

By its natural inclination power tends to perpetuate and strengthen itself. As Montesquieu said, power will expand until it is stopped. If it does not encounter any obstacle, it will constantly advance. Its own internal mechanisms lead it to be ever more profound, more absolute, and more comprehensive. It tends to free itself from all external precepts, and to constitute itself as its own ultimate *raison d'être*. *Princeps a legibus solutus* and *L'Etat c'est moi* are the classic maximalist formulae. Unrestrained power ends up subduing everything and extinguishing liberty. Authority, however, aspires to be freely recognized. It demands spontaneity and abhors coercion. Neither the thinker nor the poet wish to be forcefully heard. Authority, given over to its most unfettered dialectic, does not tend to enslave anyone. It has no interest in the acclaim of the multitude. Carried to its limits, political power does not admit a solution other than having itself killed: the revolution. Authority in contrast seeks to be petitioned. Power demands that people give themselves up, it seeks domination, while authority pursues consensus and asks that people remain at a distance.

By its end, although ethics teaches us that political power must work for justice and the common good, sociology shows that it does not automatically realize that ideal. Left to itself and decoupled from external constraints, power becomes egotistical and ultimately immoral. That is why Lord Acton declared that all power corrupted, and absolute power corrupted absolutely. It is a will to dominate implacably and without limits, and, if necessary, it will uproot, sacrifice, humiliate and destroy. The natural growth of power is egotistical, while authority is a virtue, and, in its maturity, necessarily supposes perfection. The end of authority is inherently moral. One can only speak metaphorically of immoral authorities. The real authority of an expert safe-breaker or a forger would lie in their being precision mechanics or first class engravers, not in being thieves. The egoism of authority is constructive, positive, and honest. Malignant authority is a contradiction in terms.

In reference to its passive subject, power is not rational. He who obeys it, even if he is free to do so, is primarily moved by fear. Even he who exercises it, for all his justifications, feels he has power because he has it, and that is that. He expresses himself in decisions, not in reasonings. Power becomes part of the will. Rationality is an accidental aspect, a forced addition in the actual exercise of power. Authority however exists where it is objectively recognized. "X has said it," no one has designated him, no one fears him, but he has authority. His justification is logical: He is virtuous. In his conquest of authority there is a rational strategy, since it is the search for the objective, not the subjective good. The physicist knows that his authority rests on real knowledge and discoveries. For the powerful man, sovereignty is not rational, nor for the man who suffers it, for it not usually the fruit of a systematic and necessary action, but of a concatenated series of arbitrariness and chance.

In relation to its temporal nature, power is fleeting and volatile. It is won or lost for some motive, but rarely for a real reason. The loss of power is in part a burlesque, in part a dramatic situation, that few men can completely overcome. Authority instead tends to last for a lifetime, and once gained, is not threatened in the way power is. Rather the opposite is true, and circumstances conspire to perpetuate it. If authority is lost, it is always the result of an error or of biological decadence. The man who has authority does not suffer the terrible anguish to continue in power, which is the great neurosis of the politician, and which leads him to subordinate everything, including precepts and oaths, to the maintenance of personal sovereignty. Normally political power is transitory, while authority endures. Everything passes away in this world, but few things pass so swiftly and leave such deep spiritual scars as does power. This unforgettable transitoriness of power is the best known feature of its despicable condition.

Perhaps because political power intends possession of the other man, the mass leader has come to be thought of as the hero par excellence, in spite of the fact that he has been morally classified time and again as rapacious, unjust, and cruel. It is an almost universal conviction that power ennobles, and that the highest calling is to govern. The great champion of irrationalism, which is always the philosophy of tyranny, Freidrich Nietzsche, maintained that the will for power, *Wille zur Macht*, was the great driving force of nature, the purest expression of energy. His Dionysian ethics crystalizes in the precept that the superior man must fight for his empire and that this is his supreme destiny. All this is lyric and myth. The fact that political power consists in subjugating human liberty does not dignify it. It debases it.

From its delegated origin, its coercive character, its absolutist tendency, its natural egoism, and its concomitant irrationalism, power is much less noble than the creative, peaceful, liberal, altruistic, and rationalized concept of authority. That is why the truly superior spirits, the philosopher, the scientist, the technologist, the mystic, and the poet always prefer the path of authority to that of power. And when they fall to the temptation, like Plato and Seneca, they withdraw contrite and purified. The really noble politicians are those who are given power because they have already invested themselves with authority. Developed countries entrust political power to those who have authority. Authority, more than the legitimizing of sovereignty, as the scholastics claimed, has its own inherent foundation; it is the command by those most fitted to it.

As ideologies become extinguished and politics becomes rationalized, so power becomes saturated with authority, and the coercing, absolutist, amoral and arbitrary factors scarcely come into operation. The prevailing factors are determined by authority, that is, merit, spontaneity, self-determination, common good and reason. This then is the way in which politics are progressing in our time; from ideologies to ideas, from liberty to security, from election to control, and from power to authority.

From Enthusiasm to Consensus

The Greek origin of the word enthusiasm means ectasis or divine transport, something close to deification or apotheosis. In mode and usage, it has come to mean an exaltation or fervent adhesion which multiplies psychic energies, brings tension to the spirit, and creates the situation for so many great gestures. But, for all its Olympian and heroic genealogy, philosophers have never been devoted to enthusiasm. Plato termed it, "a state of being outside oneself", "a deviation like an illness or like sleep", in other words, a parenthesis or inflexion. Kant grappled with the problem, and after subtle distinctions condemned it: "enthusiasm hinders the free consideration of principles and can in no way merit the acquiescence of reason". Because of this he preferred *Affektlosigeist* or phlegm. Voltaire's judgment was ever more damning: "Enthusiasm marvelously links itself to the party spirit; it is a misunderstood devotion, it is incompatible with reason, it is like wine". Why have thinkers so implacably opposed the state of mind most favored by rulers?

In the individual, enthusiasm is a vehement adhesion to something which he takes to be best. It is a positive, hopeful, and apologetic movement. It is excitement and the heightening of emotion. We find our vision restricted, and all effort concentrated: it is as if we are in the middle of a race, the pupils of the eyes fixed on the finishing line and blind to all else. The woman is more enthusiastic than the man, the adolescent more than the adult, and the primitive man more that his civilized counterpart. Enthusiasm exists in a climate of rapture and hysteria, mystical trances, romantic inspiration, political fanaticism, and totalitarian grandiloquence. The enthusiast tends to be passionate, one-sided, simple, obsessive, dogmatic. The opposite to this are balance, objectivity, a critical outlook, openness, doubt, coherence, attention to details; namely, values more strictly rational. The real starting point for philosophy is curiosity, not enthusiasm.

Impetus, a basic vital quality on which one's biological and psychic level depends, is something very different, that may apply equally to a faustian or a blessed biography. Enthusiasm deserves a poor speculative grade, and is a weakness that disqualifies intellectually. Its worth in the individual is accordingly slight.

The enthusiastic condition of the masses has always been a capital political factor. An enthusiastic people becomes more aggressive and, on occasions, more efficient; it is easier to govern because it is immune to polemical objections. It is so docile that it can be led anywhere, even to suicide. It is as if drunk, unconcerned with daily worries. Such people do not need to be kept informed: only stimulated. Enthusiastic people are not sustained by realities but by simple words. An enthusiastic minority can cause an adverse silent majority to socially disappear. It is not surprising that such an easy and all-embracing tactic like enthusiasm should be continually used; a great part of the history of humanity has to do with the creation and channeling of enthusiasm. This formula also had its doctrinaires: Marx, Sorel, or in our days Sartre, whose jumbled and repetitive Critique of Dialectical Reason, based on the events of the French Revolution, is an exaltation of what he calls "the group in fusion" or "the group as a passion"; that is, a society that is unfettered, at boiling pitch, and revolutionary. Some would wish to take the Bastille every day.

It is questionable whether the manipulation of enthusiasms, for all its efficiency, is desirable. Three points must be borne in mind. Firstly, an enthusiastic people is an easy prey to tyranny; enthusiasm is the technique of the totalitarian government. The reason for this is obvious: It allows for personal command, the predominance of activism, the substitution of information by propaganda and of reason by illusion, the curtailment of dialogue, the perpetuation of the states of emergency, absolutism, extreme exaggeration, and the appeal to fantasy. Politics becomes rhetoric; it is literally the Nazi style.

In the second place, while enthusiasm can be a part of a conservative totalitarianism, it is more usually the instrument of revolutionary movements, for a revolution is a break with the past, a rupture of continuity, an attempt to perpetuate instability, to seek utopias, to simplify problems, and to impose violence and morality. All this is more easily achieved through passion, in an atmosphere of enthusiasm.

In the third place, collective enthusiasm is more likely where socioeconomic development is slow. The obstacles to mass enthusiasm are institutions, the raising of the cultural level, the rationalization of the political conscience, the technification of the administration, the consolidation of the state structure, public order, and constitutional stability. Moreover, modern means of communication have created something that was difficult to believe possible in a mass society: a bilateral, almost friendly relationship between the governor end the governed. Electrifying rabble-rousing appears comical in such circumstances. Let us try to imagine Mussolini on a television screen, while the children play around the father of the family, who is trying to watch him. Take away the Piazza of Venezia and the fervid multitude, and he appears like a caricature. It is a sociological law that, as a people become developed, they lose their capacity for collective enthusiasm.

It is a serious matter for those who prefer liberty to dictatorship, and evolution to subversion, that the politics of enthusiasm are so bound up with totalitarianism and revolution. The objection is all the stronger and is also independent from any ideological position when such politics are shown to be anachronistic and retrogressive. As a group emerges from underdevelopment, enthusiasm declines. A government that relies on oratory influences the socially deprived, and has therefore an interest in maintaining the status quo. That is its inherent danger.

The old phenomenon of the decline of an individual's enthusiasm corresponds to a similar decline on the level of societies as a whole. The 19th century European states were effusive and declaratory. The totalitarian regimes of this century took this rhetoric to its ultimate limits, and it still survives in Eastern Europe. But it is rapidly disappearing in the West.

The substitute for collective enthusiasm in a developed society is a tacit adhesion to consensus. This is not simply logical consent to a given thesis; it implies confidence and support. Consensus is relatively silent and far from being exhibitionist. Consensus is rational rather than passionate because it springs from intelligence and will, not from sentiment. Consensus is more stable than enthusiasm because it feeds on sober judgments and intimate decisions. It has no need for hot air. Consensus is pacifist, and only reacts when consistently provoked, it is neither unconditional nor absolutist. It is as difficult to create as it is to destroy. It is a permanent, sustaining factor, neither fractious nor destructive.

On the ethical plane consensus embraces traditional customs and ultimately moral norm and judicial procedures. The idea of consensus appeared with that of "what ought to be." But this, though important, is not the extent of it, for consensus is the root of all science. The first principles and basic postulates gained their strength from what the romans termed the "*consentium gentium.*"

The institutions that are founded on enthusiasm tend to be extremist and transitory. Those built upon consensus are more likely to be moderate, to maintain equilibrium, and to possess continuity. Societies are enthusiastic in inverse proportion to their level of development; consensus however is the choice of an enlightened and mature community. While enthusiasm belongs to ideologies, consensus is part of truth and virtue. What is the best in the history of humanity has been the work of the consensus of a minority of wise men, while the worst of collective crimes are perpetrated in the midst of enthusiasm. A rational society, free from ideology, needs to be moved and interested rather than drugged and fascinated. It is a conscious, not a frenzied society. The movement is from ideologies to ideas and from enthusiasm to consensus.

The Three Stages

The great historical law of positivism, freed from its pseudo-theological trammels, is confirmed in political knowledge and forms. There is a first level which is charismatic, and in which government is based on oracles and imagination. Its most ancient theoretic expression was fetishism, and its most modern ones are the divine right of kings and the commands of providence. There is a second ideological level in which myths are secularized by popularized political philosophies. Governments act based on platitudes and grand words, as exemplified by the European state of the second half of the 19th century. There is finally a third level, the scientific state, in which politics have become completely rational. This marks the end of charismas and ideologies, for politics are subjected at all levels to a scientific treatment. The change became necessary as the state was forced to undertake a wider range of activities. And also because the progress of the social sciences allows such an undertaking and provides a relatively precise conceptual system. Protopolitics excepted, social ethics, the science of government, with economics at the forefront, and the science of human behavior are disciplines that are becoming more rational, more efficient and more technical. Governors now have to be recruited from among the professionals, and not from the ranks of political dilletantes and *aficionados* to popular rhetoric. Supreme government decisions can only be confidently made if the advice of experts is followed. It is no longer licit to administer with stop-go opportunism and to abandon the solution of a problem to the chance of universal suffrage. One has to govern as one would run a factory, knowing exactly what has to be done according to the latest information.

Although slowly, positive methods are beginning to throw light on man's behavior, something that was formerly thought to be indeterminate and inexplicable. Categories and types are elaborated, and constant relationships and functions are discovered and measured. Political science is now placing new data at a statesman's disposal. The patient manipulation and observation of events in history is beginning to bear fruit. One wonders what the reaction of Vives would have been on being informed that it was possible to measure a child's capacity and the level of authoritarianism in any given character. Or how would Rousseau react to being told that it was possible to predict the result of an election, and that the discovery of a "pilot electoral District" is at hand. The small number of discoveries and the low probability level of certain sociological laws certainly indicate that all this is only a beginning; but a start has been made.

Ideologies can never form the criteria for wholesome government. Comparing them to the science of politics is like comparing an ordinary lens to an electron microscope. The crudeness and lack of precision of ideologies make them altogether inadequate to cope with the governmental decisions of today. What can liberalism or socialism say about the proper location of a development area, or the fixing of custom tariffs, or the oil prospecting, other than confused vagaries? Ideologies have had to make way for rational politics, for they are too archaic and too emotional to survive the progress of scientific knowledge. The sociologist sees the ideologue like some sort of witch-doctor for the masses. The substitution of ideologies by scientific ideas on human behavior and on the functioning of the structure of authority corresponds to the substitution of nebulous, approximate, and hypothetical concepts by clear, exact and proven ones; of metaphorical, generic and imaginary concepts by straightforward, specific and real ones. In short, the substitution of opinions by science. This is no brusque revolution, but part of the trajectory of the logos that, having started with the first man, will only end with the last. Intellectual progress relegates ideologies to the junkyard of mental curiosities.

VI. The Interiorization of Beliefs

The West is undergoing a process whereby beliefs are becoming more intimate. It is difficult to think in terms of a return to the wars of religion. The exterior manifestations of religion are diminishing, and the separation between church and state is growing. The distances between the internal conscience and the external conduct are widening, secular institutions are appearing, there is an increasing respect for the liberty of conscience, and an increasing capacity to live with men of other creeds. Religious modesty is growing and there is a spreading hostility to exhibitionist and political facts made on behalf of the church. All this implies a spontaneous and spiritual development of religion; religious sentiment is returning to its roots and becoming an intimate matter. This clear tendency has repercussions, albeit indirect ones, on the development of certain ideologies.

All the major existing religions have an inherent ethical code and therefore a series of precepts concerning mutual tolerance. As these precepts become popularized, they can take on the aspect of a new ideology, or associate themselves directly with an existing one, or they can serve as a pretext for a lay ideology to obtain ecclesiastical approval. That is why there are parties that boast religious approval and pretend to be the political arm of a religious conviction. Obviously as religion withdraws into itself, those parties claiming divine support will suffer; the process of interiorization cannot favor any form of propagandistic or political activity. The more intimate form of man's relationship with God conflicts with the development of ideologies drawing their strength from religion. Therefore, in addition to political apathy, doctrinal convergences, and the rationalization of the social sciences, we have the interiorization of beliefs as a further factor in the breakdown and dissolution of ideologies.

But the fact that certain ideological convictions are able to base themselves on religion leads to a highly suggestive and significant series of questions. What is the interdependence existing between the ideological and the religious phenomena? Are the ideologies that claim sacred origins genuine religions? Does the twilight of ideologies imply a similar process where beliefs are concerned?

The Ideological-Religious Connection

A religion is a human manner of establishing a relationship with divinity. It does not really matter whether this relationship is based on knowledge, sentiment, a sense of dependency or one of bondage. Whatever it might be, a Religion always implies an idea of God or of theology, but not necessarily one of ethics, an idea of what ought to be done. The law of Moses came after Abraham's worship, and there is an infinity of Primitive rituals that do not adopt moral positions. A religion paves the way to a relationship with God, but not necessarily with one's neighbor. In its strictest sense the religious phenomenon is an individual one: that is why there are hermits. Robinson Crusoe was able to be a mystic while ignoring the rudiments of social ethics. The superior religions do not invent a morality. They sanction and emphasize a morality that already exists. That is why members of many different faiths and even atheists are able to agree on certain fundamental commandments. There is a natural morality that is independent of the religious one. And there are many Catholics, Protestants, Muslims and deists who would subscribe to the same Aristotelian Thomist social ethic. Revelation is an act of faith, but moral order is one of rational acceptance. To confuse the religious and moral acts is very inexact and implies an inherent process of secularization that ultimately leads to contradictions such as the naturalization of the supernatural.

Essentially Christian morality does not pretend to be anything other than a system of precepts that are imperative for the human being. An ideology that appeals to moral theology does not therefore assume a religious mantle but an ethical one instead, one that can be -and in the event always has been– assumed by widely separate sectors throughout history. An ideology that flaunts its Catholicism to differentiate itself from others can have two motives: a) it might insist on those points that amount to a restrictive roman catholic interpretation of natural morality, such as the indissolubility of marriage; or b) it might seek a favorable treatment for Catholicism. The first point, by virtue of being moral, qualifies the religious position. The pretext of an actual discrepancy over the promulgation of a positive precept cannot place man's relationship with God in a parenthesis. But above all we are here concerned with situations that because they affect the private individual and the wellbeing of the community are insufficient to serve as a basis for a specific ideology; and that is why the Christian democrats have come to terms with civil divorce. The second point concerns the controversial dilemma of the neutral or confessional state. Without going any further into this thorny question, it is common knowledge that numerous eminent theologians uphold the notions of liberty of conscience and of religious neutrality within the power structure. Therefore, an ideology whose main characteristic is the religious militancy of the state can exist, but it has no right to call itself a Christian ideology to the exclusion of all others. There is not a necessary qualitative relationship between ideology and religion and this initial conclusion conditions the subsequent argument.

The Religious Content of Ideologies

Are ideologies that claim sacred origins witnesses to religiosity? The spokesmen for such ideologies are the political parties that more or less closely follow a specific creed. But these parties are not by their nature associations formed for spiritual perfectioning and are not and cannot be judged as one would a monastic order by the sanctity of their members. In fact, the religious example given by the party leaders and militants is far from being satisfactory, but this cannot be raised as a legitimate objection, for the ends of a political movement are practical and belong to the natural order. But even collectively these parties are not the civic incarnation of orthodoxy. In fact, they can never be this, for there are innumerable questions within the polity that religion and the morality sanctioned by it leave for men to settle among themselves. That is why members of the same faith can be politically divided and belong to opposing ideologies: progressive and traditionalist. But the contingencies and uncertainties of the debates are not the decisive issue. A political party moves on the level of existences not of essences, and is therefore obliged to coexist with its adversary and to constantly accept the lesser of two evils. The Christian democrat parties grew up to bridge the hiatus that theoretically and historically had come between the church and the revolution. This paradoxical destiny has led these parties into deviations and shady compromises that have proscribed them from representing true orthodoxy. Orthodoxy has been relatively more viable for the more or less utopian integrisms. It is moreover indisputable that, in the case of profoundly religious countries, such as India, there are no great parties that are founded on a sacred ideology. However, in nations where atheism has made great inroads, and where, as in the case of Italy, there is a menacing and growing Marxist party, the center of the political stage is held by a party with Christian roots. By definition a party with a confessional ideology does not constitute a testimony of genuine religiosity. And the facts correspond to the principles. One may therefore deduce that all the religiously ideological parties might disappear and yet the purity, the intensity of the individual and collective faith might still be able to increase. There is not, indeed, necessarily a connection between the existence of sacred ideologies and the level of authentic religiosity.

The Parallel

Does the twilight of ideologies imply a decline in beliefs? Is there a quantitative correlation between what is ideological and what is religious? We are here concerned with a hurried updating of the old pseudo-dilemma of reason and faith, that is, of the supposed anti-religiosity of the rationalist movements. The somewhat irrational characteristics of an ideology and of a religion and the manner in which both influence human behavior are the indices of such a possible connection. But both experience and speculative analysis give lie to such a hypothesis. Until Luther, Christianity appeared to be the imperial ideology. Yet, the extinction of the latter coincided with the splendid flowering of religiosity in the reformed church and in the counterreformation. Right up to 1789, Catholicism appeared to be part and parcel of the Ancient Regime. Yet, in the midst of the ideological hegemony of liberalism, Europe witnessed a magnificent resurgence of the Catholic faith. It appears that religion benefits when it abandons ideological pretensions.

The direct observation of individual examples is corroborated when history is generalized to a certain level of abstraction. The great religions were born in roundabout and profound ways, under conditions of almost family intimacy. A faith then matures in an esoteric, hermit-like and unworldly manner. These features are the complete antithesis of the populism, the pragmatism and vulgarization, archetypical features of the ideologic. A religious movement, because it seeks to completely bind itself to divinity, develops very differently to an ideology. There are however analogies when decadence sets in, when the internal life of a religion melts away, because religion at that point ceases to be essentially a belief in the supernatural and becomes an ideology. The kernel of religious experience is to be found in the most profound interior of the human spirit, where even introspection cannot really reach. Faith delves deep inside oneself, binding itself to one's most intimate nature in a manner that is both fragile and strong, and which is always mysterious. A belief that is however limited to outward forms is a deceptive and inert empty shell. That is why the sense of sin has got a religious potential that is entirely lacking in formal piety and even virtuous inertia. In contrast, ideologies are superficial affective and mental subproducts, masked desires tied to the present moment, and slowly evolving. The external appearance of ideologies is so decisive that what stabilizes them most in the short term is their own publicity: outside pressure and fear of being charged with opportunism. Exactly the opposite occurs with beliefs that are tranquil and reposed in their intimate retirement, but tend to outward manifestations at precisely the point where they assume the ideological trappings.

For all their partial irrationalities, religions and ideologies do not develop in a parallel fashion. The rationalist process destroys ideologies because these have a deceptive and frustrated pretension to reason. Beliefs however are not incompatible with pure speculation and have even given rise to philosophy. They are not in any danger because of this, since in the nooks and crannies of dogma there are always irrational nuclei which are inexplicable by the logos. There is not a necessary quantitative relationship between the religious and the ideological, and in practice it does not exist. In spite of all of Comte's forecasts, there was a growth of religious feeling at the height of positivism. It is foolish to forecast a decline of faith alongside the decline of ideologies, for probably the very opposite is true.

In conclusion ideologies are the parasites of religion, not their resultants. The ideological institutions that adhere to a religious creed do not represent it with any degree of purity, nor could they do so. An ideology is rather a ballast where the divine is concerned. There is therefore no cause to value negatively the interiorization of beliefs and its repercussion on the crisis of ideologies.

The Subjectivation of Culture

The interiorization of beliefs, like any other trend, however peculiar, does not arise in isolation, but within a context. This environment is the subjectivation of culture. By widening our field of observation, we gain in perspective without losing contact with our principal theme, the disappearance of ideologies. Our theme will reappear from different premises.

Up to the beginning of the 20th century western scholarship divided humanity into cultured and uncultured peoples. The most notable antecedents of this basic dichotomy can be found in the Hebrew notion of the chosen people, and the later distinction between Greeks and barbarians. This second dualism was basic to the classical world and, far from disappearing, took renewed forms as modern man made contact with the East, the New World, and Africa. A vestige of this belief is found in the still very common expression "cultured languages." For millennia culture was conceived to be the absolute whole, and the societies that had more of it were deemed to be the properly cultured societies. The leading peoples in the West constituted themselves into the inventors and definers of culture, on a moral and artistic level as well as on a scientific and technical one. When in the still recent past Japan and Turkey decided to become cultured nations, they imported even their clothes from Europe.

This presently antiquated absolutist notion of culture did not exclude, but in fact implied the notion of progress. Culture was not conceived as whole and completed, like a platonic idea, but as something that man was progressively creating. It was a movement of asymptotic approximation, hence situated within time. The fact that baroque culture was less advanced than that of the enlightenment historifies and qualifies the concept, but does not relativize it. In the drastic formulation of Eugenio D'Ors, "there has never been nor can there ever be more than one culture." But history was not being denied.

This conception began to be undermined from several flanks, and most directly by sociology and anthropology. Culture came to be defined as the sum total of the modes of life of a particular society. Given this meaning, the savage had as much culture as the civilized man. And not because the culture of the former is a preliminary stage to that of the latter. Rather, because, even supposing it to be irreducible, imperfectible and immutable, the most primitive is a culture in itself. Sociologist attempted to manipulate this concept avoiding any value-judgments. However, as soon as they went beyond the purely empirical level, qualitative comparisons arose. For example, the question was posed whether black music was better than white music, and the answers were somewhat uncertain. The methodic neutrality of the sociologist has developed into a cultural relativism and into a state of indifference to an extensive repertoire of life forms. The process has been accelerated by efforts for international understanding and the presumed equality of sovereign states. The UNESCO is one of the great promotion agencies of this subjectivization. And its famous *History of humanity* is a landmark in the task of comparing the different cultures.

For non-westerners, pluri-culturalism overcomes an inferiority complex and vindicates a group. For the westerner there is more than a mere enrichment of his knowledge of the world beyond. He experiences a partial relativization of his conception of the world. On all sides there is a process of breaking down barriers, from religion to fashion passing through art. It can no longer be claimed that the white man's tie is more civilized than a native dress or that a romantic "Lied" is superior to a Bengali wail chant, nor that French is richer than Chinese literature or Islam less noble than Calvinism.

Does this cultural relativism lead into pure and simple skepticism? I don't think so. The mutual tolerance of different cultures allows an element of choice and even of arbitrariness over habits, beliefs, and modes of life. Within this element of choice there is not, in a certain sense, any truth. Much that had aspired to be objective and that many had struggled to have recognized as such, becomes subjective. Tolerance does not extend to all that is attainable and knowledgeable; while certain positions become less rigid, others become more set in their ways. Pluriculture relativizes almost all culture in its classical sense, but at the same time it makes the rational and scientific nucleus still more absolute. There are no options in exact knowledge. Nor is there a simultaneous relativism with respect to the basic interpersonal duties. That is why, in contrast to the 19th century, the backward countries today are able to preserve not a few of their intrinsic customs. Nevertheless, they do have to submit docilely to the despotism of the rational knowledge so far developed in the West, because this knowledge has a pretension to objective truth. Science is the dogmatic aspect of present day culture, and the rest is debatable.

Pluriculture is not free of negative implications. One of them is its role as a spur to nationalism. But once the interchangeable and optional character of local traditions and cultural idiosyncrasies is realized, then the process of cosmopolitan convergence is underway. Moreover, it is tendentiously reactionary to massively promote little known or nearly extinct languages, as in the case of Hebrew. The multiplicity of languages is, socially speaking, a hindrance. One would hope that in the future the understanding of humanity will be achieved through the universal language of science. The vast majority of vernacular languages will stand for self-determination and isolation rather than cooperation and communication. The subjectification of culture broadens one's personal range of experiences and multiplies the possibilities of realizing oneself individually. The standardization of reason is compensated by the almost unlimited diversification of culture. Today the opening up to all of the totality of the different ways of life, the most exotic included, increases the options for the individual and makes self-determination so much easier, even for the least original. The "logos" alone demands universality but in the surrounding heterogeneous hinterland there is great scope for the intimate.

Alongside this concurrent relativization and absolutism, there exists in the polity a corresponding double phenomenon. It consists of the twilight of ideologies, and so of similarly arbitrary positions, as well as of the primacy of the empirical and efficient element in the governmental programs. Pluriculture infuses irony into much of our conception of the world, while at the same time making the rigorous more radical. In the same way, the process of deideologization reveals the inconsistent facets in the traditional polity, while emphatically strengthening its rational core.

VII. Economic Development

Humanization and Industrialization

The famous controversy over technology, which has occupied the cream of the European intellectuals for over half a century, has always appeared Byzantine to me. Reason is what is noblest on earth, science is the very product of reason, and technology is applied science. It is a very clear progression. Obviously, technological breakthroughs such as the splitting of the atom can be used evilly, but this is true of everything in man's experience, from truth to beauty, from liberty to intellect, from gold to silex.

Technology is as old as Adam, but only in the last century did it progress sufficiently to be able to transform the life of the masses. That moment has now come: two thirds of the increase of the national income is due to technology as opposed to natural resources. Technology both liberates man from servile work and supplies him with goods and services that were formerly reserved to only the most privileged minorities. The quality of western man's life is constantly being raised, and the possibilities of the exploitation of nature appear to be unlimited. This prodigious revolution is neither materialistic, nor superficial, nor inhuman. It is the creation of reason, like philosophy and mathematics. It is also the creation of will and of impetus, like heroism and art. And it is profoundly humanizing for the masses. Certain privileged existences such as those of Seneca and Goethe will be more difficult to lead in the approaching era of technology. But against this, the inhuman conditions suffered for millennia by the universal proletariat will disappear. Technology does not promote the revolt of the masses; it promotes them to a more human level. This has enormous sociological consequences.

Already in the old *Primum vivere deinde philosophari* there is a vague anticipation of the precise data on the evolution of consumption that modern analysis has revealed. There is a priority of essential needs and consequently a hierarchy of goods is built up. The starving man does not spend his resources buying a book any more than the naked purchases a jewel. The primary necessities are satisfied first, and the superior ones later. Those sectors of humanity to whom food, clothing, housing and sexuality constitute an absorbing problem will only in exceptional cases practice those activities that require leisure time, and which are peculiar to man. Misery insulates a man and degrades him spiritually and intellectually. It is a motor to anarchy, animalization and materialism, and pulls us back towards prehistory. Well-being is socially the condition of the opposite. That is why, although technology is the product of reason, it makes possible the exercise of reason itself.

Aside from permitting the satisfaction of needs, technology has analogous repercussions on production. Around 1860 the value of the national income in France was as follows: agriculture 58%, industry 21%, and services, teaching etc. 21%. A century later the respective distribution was 14%, 41% and 45%. The products of the so-called tertiary sector, services, teaching, hygiene, liberal professions and so on, which were formerly a fifth of the total, amount now to nearly half. A second example further illustrates this universal tendency. In Sweden between 1860 and 1930 the number of people engaged in liberal professions rose eight times while the population did not even double. It would therefore appear that considerably more intellectual life is being produced.

Economic development dignifies man and turns, among innumerable other secondary effects, the attentions of the masses towards productive work, and so separates them from political battles. Simultaneously it raises the number of property owners, increasing social responsibility and stability. Both the proletarian and the aristocrat become bourgeois; classes are drawn together as do their interests, so that different groups establish solidarity among each other, political programs resemble each other, and the polarization of conflicting claims is overcome. All this accelerates the disappearance of ideologies. Moreover, the raising of the standards of living entails the decrease of illiteracy, the intellectualization of activities, and the general raising of the average man's power of reasoning. As the level of rationality is raised, so passion and gut-reactions disappear. Simplicity and sheeplike docility are replaced by critical faculties and understanding, and so the times seem set against the proliferation of ideologies.

Technology and economic development, the most evident characteristics of our time and the determinants of our future environment, are factors of egalitarianism and rationalism. There is an inverse relation between ideology and development. That is why politics is more ideological in Albania than in Belgium, or more so in Britain than in the United States. The most fruitful ground for ideologies today lie with the emergent African nations, that are intellectually, politically, and economically backward. The issues that some time back shook Europe, nationalism, racism, xenophobia, class, and religious conflict are reappearing in African society. Such ideologies are localized, in addition to being anachronistic, in a way that the great western ideologies of the 19th century were not. This would appear to show that the rule of ideologies is a form of social primitivism.

Retarding Factors

The disappearance of ideologies, initiated in the West but not yet apparent in other areas, is a slow process because it is linked to the fundamental transformation of the social structures. Tradition and the inertia that it causes is the first great retarding factor. For the past one and a half centuries politics have been built up around ideological juxtapositions. It is therefore almost a mental habit to think of the polity in terms of socialism or liberalism. The mark of certain ideologies is so old, so extensive, and so deep, that they attempt to identify themselves with national traditions, and so become historical constants. This is true of the principles of 1789 in France. In such cases, the process of deideologisation appears as a partial desubstantiation of the nation. The inherent relativism of revolutions explains that the most subversive and renovating ideologies, having once imposed themselves, become traditions. Marxism is already a tradition in the Soviet Union. Contrary to what is supposed, the ideological position is the reactionary one, not the anti-ideological one. For the "ideocracy", for the politics of rational ideas, the notions of conservatism and progressivism have scarcely any meaning. The yardstick is neither antiquity, nor novelty, but truth and efficiency. If it is anything at all, science is inherently progressive, because it is in perpetual motion toward objective goals. Ideologies however, even those that herald the most innovations, tend to become crystalized. When they undergo the process of evolution and convergence, they decline, and socialism is a case in point. The rational politician, like the scientist, must be ready at any moment to abandon a hypothesis or a method and to admit a breakthrough or a rectification. The ideologue, in contrast stays close to his plan. Ideologies that have become established tend to preserve themselves intact, and so become desperately conservative. The ideological polarities are so socially resistant that they continue to exist even when the realities on which they have based themselves have disappeared. What gave rise to the terms "right" and "left" disappeared 25 years ago, and theoreticians have abandoned such an equivocal distinction. The formula, nevertheless, constantly reappears, perhaps with metamorphosed meanings. But, in spite of its age, its lack of validity and of meaning, it exists all the same. The inertia caused by tradition works in favor of established ideologies and, as with everything else, only the sustained efforts of a few will cause a flexibility and a rationalization in the collective conscience.

It is not only habits and traditions that act as brakes, as retarding factors. Institutions also play an important role because ideologies claim their support as much as that of the average man. There are parties that are purely instrumental or personalist, hence having practically no ideological content. They are normally transitory but can be permanent, as is the case of the Democrat and Republican parties in the United States. However, many of the major modern political parties are ideological. Their stability is based on their loyalties to fundamental positions and their strength is a more or less compact mass of believers. These parties are active promoters of ideologization. There are some that are so radical that they prefer extinction to evolution, which indicates that the principle of essential conservatism can be stronger than that of existential preservation. Others give way to the implacable demands of reality. The disagreements between liberals and socialists are not mere opportunistic exercises; they are adaptations of something prior and more profound: the alteration of the social structures. Nevertheless, political parties are undergoing a crisis, as is notorious in their country of origin and adoption, France. The causes lie in the incapacity of political parties to carry out the principle of representation and their lack of efficiency in matters of government. Internal inbreeding and political instability are the twin root causes of the decline of party politics: and it is the ideologically based parties that are hardest hit. Only the transitory, ad hoc groupings appear to have any future. Such a decline weakens the retarding action that parties might exercise, and so ultimately amounts to yet another factor in the ideological crisis.

The third major factor lies with the politicians who continue 19th century uses. Right at the start of the democratic state, the ideologues gained ruling positions; as the masses became something more tangible and concrete, there came a flowering of local political bosses and demagogues. But the first of these were ephemeral figures, and the second became part and parcel of their own slogans. That is why, in spite of changes, the professional politician has for a century and a half been confused with the ideologue. Those who have spent most of their public life in those routines are unable to change. They will continue to draw their inspiration from ideologies and place all their political action within the ideological context. The disappearance of this generation will not mean the end of the species. Ideologism retains a pragmatic virtue that gains it adepts. An ideology is something simple and quickly learnt; it is the universal panacea, the recipe for all occasions, the master key. It is rather like a political Aladdin's lamp: rub it lightly and the solution will appear. What is to be done? The demo-liberal ideology answers immediately: obey the majority. The Marxist also has his answer: serve the interests of the proletariat, and so on. With such ready knowledge, political dedication becomes a happy coincidence of vocation and opportunity. It is not properly speaking a knowledge, although ideologies attempt to give a theoretic appearance to simplified topics, interests and pseudo-ideas. It is difficult to think of anything more comfortable or as egalitarian; in such a situation the differences between a government and a gathering of friends in their club appear as purely accidental. How is an organic law of the state drafted? How is a university reformed? How is the credit ceiling established? What industries should be promoted? It is only natural that all those who have no knowledge of public law, who are neither pedagogues, economist nor financiers should abandon any attempt to rationalize politics and turn to ideologies. It would appear obvious that previous studies are required in order to solve a differential equation, to operate on a retina, to construct a bridge or to defend a libel case. The ideologues however insist that to solve the complex problems of state administration it is sufficient to have a simple and to an extent self-taught recipe. The worst of it is that there are several conflicting recipes. It is only to be expected that those with little knowledge of the social sciences should disguise their ignorance with ideological trappings. They are numerous and their retarding effect is considerable. Their opportunities depend on the masses. As these discover that there are experts in the different actors of public life, so the ideologues will fall into oblivion and be generally discredited as quacks were not long ago.

But among the several retarding factors, perhaps the most important and widespread is man's instinct for play. In contrast to work, which is fatiguing and a means to an end, play is an agreeable activity, indulged in for its inherent pleasure, rather than for any particular result. Play is deemed such, not so much because of the nature of the activity, but because of the manner and the state of mind in which it is undertaken. In this way politics, while in itself a serious matter, has had for the present-day western man a sporting dimension. This has hardly been examined, but the analogies between the rhetorical exercise that constitutes public life, and a game are abundant and strong. In politics, as in sport, there is free and voluntary participation, there are rules that are easily learnt, innumerable combinations, a competitive tension, the risk of defeat and the possibility of victory. Politics allows for the formation of teams, it is a distraction from professional life, there is an implicit factor of fortuitous uncertainty, there is a margin of deception and astuteness, and it does not constitute a means for earning a living. There is moreover in rhetorical politics, as in sport, a certain conventional transformation of reality: roles are divided among the participants, values are understood and there are fictitious assumptions and charades. In short it is a world apart, a sham, fantastic and arbitrary. And finally in ideological politics, as in sport, there is an element of catharsis, a release of superfluous energy, a sentiment of uselessness, and above all a determination to be entertained. When politics becomes a spontaneous, improvised, varied and competitive activity, when it is also an interesting and secondary one, embarrassing, astute, gratuitous, and transfiguring, expensive, evasive and enjoyable, it must be placed within the specific coordinates of sport. Because man has a tendency, an impulse, an instinct towards play -*spieltrieb*- it is natural that he should not wish to withdraw from political activity. This of course depends upon the polity being understood rhetorically or ideologically. When politics is a strict knowledge and when the exercise of it is a true labor, then it is very far from being a game. And such is the politics of the scientific age upon which we are embarking. The defining characteristics of this new dimension are completely opposed to the concept of a game. Politics here becomes a regulated, professional, specialized and group activity, it is exact, principled, true, and remunerative, realistic, pragmatic, and sober, objective and labored. There is nothing agreeable about it; there is only the strenuous interaction of precise mechanisms. Play politics is doubtless much more fun than its scientific counterpart, and if only for this reason, there will always be those who prefer it. But as man becomes more rational to the extent of separating and distinguishing play from work, imagination from reality, and infantilism from adulthood, and as he learns to contrast what is superfluous and useless from what is necessary and practical, so leisure and business will receive their separate, distinct dues. Each day it will be more difficult to play with serious matters, and politics is by its very nature serious.

The inertia caused by habit and tradition, the ideological parties, the rhetorical political leaders and the playful conception of politics are the four major factors that retard the rationalization process of the polity. Nowadays they act as brakes on the latter's advance but, in the end, they will give way. At present the great dialectical barrier of reaction consists in the farcical denunciation of the supposed "dangers of dehumanization and technocracy." But this is pure sophistry; it is ideologies that are primitive and magical. Political science and government with the greatest possible reason are what is most progressive and most efficient and, by virtue of this, what is most human.

VIII. Conclusion

A New Ideal

The twilight of ideologies implies neither the disappearance of all ideals nor political apathy. A logical and factual analysis according to definitions as well as events will illustrate this.

Conceptually, doubts and ambiguities are possibly the result of the etymological similarity of the words ideologies and ideals, both having their roots in the Greek *eidos*. But these two words have different meanings. Ideologies are modern products, conditioned by historical circumstances. In contrast, ideals, for example justice, have always existed; they are pure and optimal goals that do not depend on historical circumstances, and are held by the wise man and the simple man alike. Ideologies can disappear, while ideals continue to exist, for while a man can live without pseudo-ideas, he cannot live without objectives or models, or more exactly, without exemplary causes.

Historically the ambiguity has more of a basis, for since the 19th century ideologies have usually functioned as collective ideals, and have at times been the rational for national undertakings. One wonders whether, as ideologies become extinguished, contemporary nations will lose their *raison d'être* and impulse.

There are numerous motives behind the behavior of a group or an individual, but this is not true of nations. A statesman's imagination is considerably less fertile than one is led to believe. Virtually all the ideals that have moved the ancient, the medieval and the modern state fall into one of three categories: independence, imperialism, or faith. The first two, although dignified by ethical or aesthetic elaborations, are usually in substance based on material and selfish interests: autocracy or domination. Apostolic undertakings, however, while sometimes a cover for expansionism, have an inherently generous and spiritual foundation. Up to the time of the Enlightenment, nations hardly knew of any ideals other than those of emancipation, hegemony or crusades. The French Revolution secularized existence and, through the Declaration of the Rights of man in 1789, created a new historic stimulus. It was no longer a question of struggling against foreign domination, or of imposing a similar domination on a neighbor, nor was it one of preaching a revealed dogma; it involved applying a lay doctrine. The first ideologies, liberalism and counter-revolutionism, were followed by socialism, communism, and fascism. Clearly, in the modern age, ideologies joined ideals, and this explains the last century and a half in the West.

The flagrant decadence of ideologies takes place when the wars of religion were over, and coincides with the universal condemnation of imperialism, and the consummation of nearly all the independence struggles. Will this virtual liquidation of traditional objectives lead to social apathy and ultimately to the stagnation of communal life? The ideals of the past are certainly declining, but this does not mean the extinction of a conscience of a concrete common good capable of generating a forceful collective action. What happens is that the psychological elements become increasingly more rational and less debased by prejudices and simplicities. There is a new ideal in the world that is neither nationalist nor confessional nor ideological; the target of all states, from the youngest to the most powerful is development. Incredible tasks are undertaken at the latter's behest: The superpowers indulge in space programs, while the smaller states embrace heavy industry. The all-encompassing drive of the developmental undertaking makes it humanity's prime-mover in its atomic age.

Development is not a new ideology as doubtlessly the remaining ideologues will claim in a final desperate sophism. It is, like justice, an ideal that has always been present in humanity, but which has never before been so collectively desired, nor so possible in the short term. As such, it does not have a program in the manner of an ideology, for it is neither a utopia nor a myth. It is a planned project that cannot degenerate into rhetorical verbosity, for it has to be rigorously applied and based on facts.

The idea of development that obsesses nations today appears to be particularly emphatic over "useful" values and this economic bias has led some to isolate two dangers: spiritual atrophy, and materialism. I believe this attitude is the result of a fragmentary and superficial understanding of the reality, and rests on the reactionary hypothesis that the intellect is a dehumanizing factor, and that science conflicts with life. This is simply not so. "Prehistoric man has been transformed into the intelligent being of today by reason and the supreme products of the mind. The scientific disciplines, medicine, law, mathematics have contributed more to our survival than passions and instincts". Development gives enormous potential to spiritual possibilities; it replaces manual labor by mental processes and so allows for progressive intellectualization; it liberates man from the basic preoccupations of existence, and so permits superior activities; it lessens the hours of work and so gives more time for contemplation, meditation, and creation. Along with greater development there are more liberal professions, more leisure time, more art, more science, in short less muscular, instinctive day to day life, and a greater unfurling of the spirit.

As far as religiosity is concerned, experience shows that civilized man is no further from God than primitive man, and that the genuine religious phenomenon is immune to rationalism. Little could be said for believers, if, in order to retain their faith, they had to return to prehistory and ignorance. The presumed incompatibility between philosophy and revelation is a trap into which many have fallen. The greatest dialectical triumph of atheism has been to infuse in certain religious spirits a fear of reason, although this is the most divine aspect of man. It is on all counts a cheap argument.

Authentic development is much more than simply altering circumstances and modifying our environment in order to make it more comfortable and pleasing. It consists also in internal perfectioning of man, in the maturation of the supreme faculties of logic, ethics and aesthetics. Development, while accelerating the processes of invention, production, and the distribution of goods, creates in men a desire to pursue the logos. Development is not only the consolidation of physical progress; it is the sublimation of human existence in all its dimensions.

Societies that are freed from ideologies do not lack an ideal. The contrary is true; the imprecise, utopian, contradictory and scarcely yielding ideologies are replaced by rigorous, viable, coherent, and efficient projects. Development is an ideal that corresponds to an ideocracy or to a "logoarchy." Development, the triumph over passions, is the spur that will urge humanity on to new heights of refinement and well-being. Development is not another name for materialism. It is the humanism of reason.

Assessment

Ideologies, like customs, are born, develop, decline, and die. The symptoms of their decline are patently clear in the most developed nations of the West. Let us finally and briefly refer back to them.

First. Electoral abstentionism, the decline of party politics, the disappearance of the doctrinaire press, the depolitization of leisure time and the dehumanization of the state are at the same time both cause and effect of the reduced interest of the citizens on political matters. Power does not rivet the attention of the average man as it did once; he is concerned with other things. Political apathy is an important witness to the process of deideologization.

Second. When two opposing ideologies tend to merge, both are on the way to dissolution. Today socialism has renounced the class struggle and the total nationalization of the means of production, and accepts commercial competition and democratic procedures. For its part, liberalism has abandoned its individualist dogmas and has substituted the principle of representation by that of administrative control, taking for its own the concepts of economic planning and the social function of property. Communism is becoming westernized and bourgeois, while capitalism preaches peaceful coexistence and the proscription of the preventive war. Nationalism is engulfed by the currents of continental unity. On every level there is a convergence and ultimately a weakening of ideologies.

Third. Social ethics is a discipline that has attained the highest levels of theoretic perfection. The government of people has become a complex matter, whose overriding concern is economic promotion; it is no longer a question of providing simply for law and order. But because the material advance of a society depends above all on the progress of the pure and applied sciences, the administration becomes a center of highly specialized scientific research. New ground is being broken in the formulation of sociological laws, and it is now possible to know the statistical behavior of certain groups. In summary, ethics, the administration, and politics become rational. This means the substitution of the ideologue by the expert, and of ideologies by physico-mathematical, economic, and social laws.

Fourth. Religions are becoming purer, less pragmatic, less political. They are losing their temporal interests. The separation between what is intimate and what is public, between the administrative and the confessional is growing. Liberty of conscience is uppermost, and beliefs are becoming interiorized. While there is a new interest in the divine, ideologies can no longer tie themselves to a religion or a lay creed, and so lose their securest mooring posts. Religions themselves, in the midst of a process of purification and rationalism, either become genuine and rigorous, or disappear. Either way they cease to exist as ideologies.

Fifth. Our time is marked by economic development that, far from dehumanizing society, dignifies individuals, intellectualizes them, increases the sense of solidarity and responsibility; the utilitarian interest of the masses is enveloped in productive work, and classes and interests are brought together. As a result, ideologies lose their most important *raisons d'être* and exert influence only in the most underdeveloped areas. In spite retarding factors such as reluctance to change, the continued endurance of ideological parties and old style rhetorical politicians, the rapid and determined existence of mental and material structures deprive ideologies of their cardinal points of reference.

Ideologies are declining, and where historical evolution has been greater, they are now no more than a shadow. The most profound and defining tendencies of the age are opposed to them. It is not a question of the classical ideologies needing renovation. The point is that every ideology is inherently an imperfect logical instrument, a concept of terrible simplicity that is completely inadequate to resolve the arduous and specialized political questions of our age, and particularly those that are posed by the demands of socioeconomic development.

Political realities are very complex, and it is often difficult to find one's way. But the situation is not that different from the realities of physics or biology, and yet no one turns to alchemy or sorcery for enlightenment. We are at the juncture of a more human and rational understanding of politics, and government is altogether something too serious to be left to the ideologues. The best way of accelerating the process is not to meet the adversary in his own territory, in other words, not to debate endlessly the hackneyed arguments, but to modify conditions to the extent that ideologies cease completely to exist. It is enough to draw attention to events, to stimulate the rationalization of political knowledge, to interiorize one's emotions, and to intensify cultural and economic development. This is the task of tomorrow's men; they have to substitute ideologies by rigorous ideas, fitting to the specification of the new frontiers. The state of the future is the "ideocracy" or the "logoarchy."

Books by Gonzalo Fernández de la Mora

- *Paradoja*, (*Paradox;* novel) Madrid, 1944, 178 pages.
- *Laina*, (novel) 1944, nonvenal, Madrid, 1994, 76 pages.
- *Ortega y el 98* (*Ortega and the generation of 1898*), ed. Rialp, Madrid, 1961, 266 pages.

  Ortega y el 98 (*Ortega and the generation of 1898*), 2nd ed. extended, Rialp, 1963, 298 pages.

  Ortega y el 98 (*Ortega and the generation of 1898*), 3d ed. Newly extended, Rialp, Madrid, 1979, 256 pages.

- *Pensamiento español*, (*Spanish thought*) 1963. From Azorín to Zubiri, Rialp, Madrid, 1964, 286 pages.

- *El crepúsculo de las ideologías* (*The twilight of ideology)*, Rialp, Madrid, 1965, 172 pages.

  El crepúsculo de las ideologías (*The twilight of ideology)*, 2° edition, extended, Zig-Zag, Santiago de Chile, 1968, 190 pages.

  El crepúsculo de las ideologías (*The twilight of ideology)*, 3ª ed., extended, Zig-Zag, Santiago de Chile, 1968, 192 pages.

  El crepúsculo de las ideologías (*The twilight of ideology)*, 4ª ed., further extended, Andina, Buenos Aires, 1970, 144 pages.

  El crepúsculo de las ideologías (*The twilight of ideology)*, 5ª ed., further extended, Salvat, Barcelona, 1971, 180 pages.

  El crepúsculo de las ideologías (*The twilight of ideology)*, 6ª ed., extended, Edicol, Bogotá, 1974, 190 pages.

  Crepuscle de les ideologies (*The twilight of ideology)*, Catalan translation by R. Bech, Dopesa, Barcelona, 1972, 168 pages.

  To Lycophos ton Ideologion (*The twilight of ideology)*, Greek translation by K. Tsiropoulos, ed. Philon, Atenas, 1973, 164 pages.

  O Crepúsculo das Ideologias (*The twilight of ideology)*, Portuguese translation by H. Barrilaro, Ulissea, Lisboa, 1973, 206 pages.

El crepúsculo de las ideologías (*The twilight of ideology*), 7ª ed. revised, Espasa Calpe, 1986, 224 pages.

El crepúsculo de las ideología (*The twilight of ideology.* Critical edition, notes and preliminary study by Carlos Goñi. Georg Olms Verlag, Hildesheim, 2003, 203 pages.

Il crepusculo delle ideologie (*The twilight of ideology*), Italian translation, Nuove Idee, 2005, Roma, 205 pages.

- *Pensamiento español,* (Spanish thought) *1964.* From Unamuno to D´Ors, Rialp, Madrid, 1965, 304 pages.

- *Pensamiento español,* (Spanish thought) *1965.* From Ortega to Nicol, Rialp, Madrid, 1966, 344 pages.

- *Pensamiento español,* (Spanish thought) *1966.* From Marañón to López Ibor, Rialp, Madrid, 1967, 462 pages.

- *Pensamiento español,* (Spanish thought) *1967.* From Castro to Millán Puelles, Rialp, Madrid, 1968, 408 pages.

- *Pensamiento español,* (Spanish thought) *1968.* From Amor Ruibal to Zaragüeta, Rialp, Madrid, 1969, 452 pages.

- *Pensamiento español,* (Spanish thought) *1969.* From Sanz del Río to Morente, Rialp, Madrid, 1971, 380 pages.

- *Del Estado ideal al Estado de razón (from Utopia to government by reason)*, Academia de Ciencias Morales y Políticas, Madrid, 1972, 130 pages.

- *La partitocracia (Partitocracy)*, Gabriela Mistral, Santiago de Chile, 1976, 180 pages.

  La partitocracia (Partitocracy), 2ⁿᵈ edition extended, Instituto de Estudios Políticos, Madrid, 1977, 308 pages.

- *El Estado de obras (Government of works)*, Doncel, Madrid, 1976, 416 pages.

- *La Constitución contemporánea (the contemporary constitution)*, in collaboration with J.M. Bordaberry et al., ed. Universitaria, Santiago de Chile, 1980, 284 pages.

- *La envidia igualitaria (Egalitarian envy)*, Planeta, Barcelona, 1984, 256 pages.

  Egalitarian envy, extended, English translation by A. T. de Nicolás, Paragon, New York, 1987, 208 pages.

  Der gleichmacherische Neid (Egalitarian envy), Extended, German translation by P. Matthes, Matthes & Seitz, Munich, 1987, 274 pages.

La envidia igualitaria (Egalitarian envy), prologue by Pedro Carlos González Cuevas, Áltera, Madrid, 2011, 270 pages.

- *Los teóricos izquierdistas de la democracia orgánica (The left wing theorists of organic democracy)*, Plaza & Janés, Barcelona, 1985, 216 pages.

- *Los errores del cambio (The blunders of our political change)*, Plaza & Janés, Barcelona, 1986, 256 pages.

  Los errores del cambio (The blunders of our political change), 2nd to 6th Plaza & Janés, Barcelona, 1987, 256 pages.

- *Filósofos españoles del siglo XX (20th century Spanish philosophers)*, Planeta, Barcelona, 1987, 216 pages.

- *Río arriba. Memorias (Upstream, memoirs)*, Planeta, Barcelona, 1995, 360 pages.

  Río arriba. Memorias (Upstream, memoirs), 2nd ed. revised, Planeta, Barcelona, IV-1995, 360 pages.

  Río arriba. Memorias (Upstream, memoirs), 3d ed. newly revised, Planeta, Barcelona, V-1995, 360 pages.

- *El hombre en desazón (Man in distress)*, Nobel, Oviedo, 1997, 377 pages.

- *El buho de Minerva. Pliegos razonalistas (Minerva's owl. Considerations on reasonalism)*. unpublished

www.ingramcontent.com/pod-product-compliance
Lightning Source LLC
Chambersburg PA
CBHW050239270326
41914CB00041BA/2050/J